GOLD
IN THEM HILLS

BEING AN IRREVERENT HISTORY
OF THE GREAT 1849 GOLD RUSH

PHIL STONG

Doubleday & Company, Inc., Garden City, New York, 1957

Library of Congress Catalog Card Number 57–6293

GOLD IN THEM HILLS

PART 1

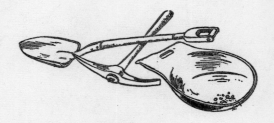

During the two most adventurous years of the Gold Rush, 1849 and 1850, Bancroft estimates that the average earnings of the California gold miner were about $600 a year. This is calculated on a population of about 100,000 in 1850 and a shipment of $41,273,600 that year.

These figures do not "jibe" nor does the estimated population agree with the U. S. Census Report of 1850, 92,597; the answer to the larger estimate being that the returns were carelessly made and the city of San Francisco and the counties of Santa Clara and Contra Costa did not turn up in the enumeration at all—the figures were lost somewhere. Indeed, Rodman Paul, the best modern historian of the Rush thinks the population may have been even 10,000 greater than Bancroft's estimate of 100,-000. (Theodore Hittell guesses a total of 150,000, which is probably generous.)

The guess, well supported, that the average miner earned $600 rather than the apparent $412.74, rests on the fact that not everyone in California was a gold miner, that a good deal of dust must have come to rest in cracks in the barroom floor and other places unlikely for recovery and accounting, and the third fact that the population of California was extremely mobile. A good many miners paused briefly and went home again, or took other employments, to be replaced by other people who could not live in Gold Rush country on $600 a year, either.

There was substantially more gold dug than ever reached the reports. Every successful miner saved enough nuggets or dust to make a watch case, a watch charm, a ring for his wife or his sweetheart or himself; my Grandfather, George Crawford Duffield, himself carried several thousand dollars in dust to the Philadelphia mint on his way back to Iowa, and also several thousand for a friend who had died of *The* fever, cholera, to his people in Ohio. Millions of dollars never appeared in any accounting. There are undoubtedly numbers of small treasures still lying around in California and along all the routes east, which are unreported.

The $600 would not have supported a California miner for more than a few months, but in the beginnings rough labor was worth $20 a day, during the productive season, and this would keep body and soul together and furnish an opportunity for a man to lay up enough of a stake to go out on his own.

Bancroft has an amusing but quite impossible story of the eccentric miner who went back East during the winter to see the towns. He noted that people stared at him in his miner's outfit, so he threw away his old beaten felt slouch hat and bought a fine high hat. Then they stared more than ever and he decided it must be his whiskers—they were quite common at the time, though not as common as they became after the Civil War; the kind of whiskers '49ers wore were, by some great mercy, never common outside the Fields, except in the American backwoods.

So the miner went to a Broadway barbershop and had a shave. On its conclusion he asked the barber if he would take his whiskers for the shave. The barber said that he would prefer his quarter.

"Then I asked him for a pan and I washed $25 worth of dust out of them right in front of his face. You ought to seen his face."

This is a valid commentary on the hygiene of the time and place but otherwise it would have strained the credulity of the White Queen, who could believe a dozen impossible things before breakfast.

Even so, for the cost of even the hungriest and raggedest living in the Fields—and the great majority of the miners were usually hungry and nearly always magnificently ragged, unshorn and dirty—the estimate seems cruelly low, but the facts were quite as cruel.

One fact upon which nearly every writer on the early days of the Rush is agreed is that more than 90 per cent of the Argonauts or '49ers would have done much better to remain in Vermont or Illinois or Missouri plowing or peddling or preaching or whatever they were doing before the fever struck them.

The Committee on Mines and Mining of the Senate of the Fifty-second Congress came just short in its report of saying that it would have been better for everyone if the virtually useless yellow metal had never been invented:

"In any other vocation in life so large a percentage of loss would destroy the industry. But the great prizes occasionally won inspire the ambition and incite the hopes of a race of men naturally adventurous; and so the work goes on and the business will continue with various successes and failures so long as precious metals are used as money. But, in the opinion of your Committee, mining for the precious metals has been and always will be prosecuted at great loss, sacrifice and toil."

This was the promised reward for a bitter voyage by land or sea or both, cruel and incessant labor, almost uninterrupted disappointment and a brutalization which generally compared with that of the serf ages of Middle Europe. Some thirty or fifty thousand people—for the statistical resources of the situation leave the estimate that broad—scattered their bones from the Missouri River to the last range of the Sierra Nevadas and over the desired land itself, some at the tip of South America where they ended their enterprise nearer the South Pole than either San Francisco or Boston.

That the participants were adventurous, as the Committee said, is a monstrous understatement. Only a handful of these people, of the Americans, knew more about getting gold than they had read in handbooks, largely written by people who had read an article in some encyclopedia. There were a few semi-skilled miners from the Carolinas and Georgia which had produced noticeable amounts of gold.

Otherwise, the art of mining was largely limited to a few Chilenos, Germans, Russians, and various nationalities which had had a little experience with washing gold. The art of pioneering was even more rare—here the new midwesterners from Tennessee to Iowa were accomplished—but the two necessary talents were virtually never observed in the same person.

However, every circumstance was calculated to encourage the emigration. In the background was the Industrial Revolution which had reduced Europe to a Poor Farm, in all its lower strata of population. It did not hit the United States so hard because the country had the advantage of unlimited territories, to which a man with very few resources beyond good health could escape from the crushing rule of the steam machines and the new age of trade, which, in most of Europe, had reduced the lower half or two thirds of the population to desperate poverty.

The discomforts of these drastic changes in world economies, ruinous to heavily populated Europe, merely squeezed America out at the edges and in the thirty or forty first years of the nineteenth century the country had established a solid and often very prosperous settlement all along the Ohio River Valley and in the East Central regions of the more proximate parts of the Mississippi Valley.

This was very well for the settling fathers but for the settling sons, who had weaned on jerky in log cabins, dressed in moccasins and buckskin breeches before their teens and brought down their first deer about the same time, the arrival of a completed civilization furnished a very drab prospect indeed, especially about the two hundredth time they had heard their daddies, sitting beside the new parlor stove, tell some yarn that began with, "Now, when I first come here——."

Besides, there was always a surplus of sons, since the settlers were a vigorous people and planned families were an unheard-of idea at the time. This was all right for the oldest of the sons, but the younger ones had to root for a career and the easiest way to do that was to move on west unless one had some unusual inclination for the professions. To all of these young men, accustomed to a rough and self-reliant life, the new gold fields were a seeming godsend.

The percussive detail which sent thousands of young men flooding to California was certainly the Mexican War. About 30,000 of the young farm hands of the United States had "seen the elephant" and walked in the halls of Montezuma, so-called. It had been a highly successful war, though except for a few brisk encounters like Molino del Rey and Chapultepec it had been more a parade than a war, properly speaking. It was most satisfactory because all of Europe had laid its bets on the highly trained, or at least highly decorative, troops of Santa Anna as against the rawboned volunteers of old "Fuss and Feathers" Winfield Scott.

Every engagement was watched by British, French, and Prussian observers waiting comfortably to see the brash young Americans get their lumps. They never did.

"What do you do with a mob," inquired one Prussian observer, "composed of half-trained and half-uniformed men, whose commanding officer's idea of a military order is to bawl, 'Give the bastards hell, boys!'—whereupon they storm an unassailable fortified height and take it forthwith?"

What they saw was a gymnasium boxer trying to lick a grizzly bear. At Chihuahua the polite Europeans were appalled to see the Yankees beating the Mexicans up with rocks when the fighting got too uncomfortably hand-to-hand to fool with swords and rifle butts and reloading a revolver would have taken too much time.

At the end of the war the United States canceled $3,000,000 in debts and gave the Mexicans $15,000,000 for nothing but Arizona, New Mexico, and California—still this was rather generous treatment for an enemy which had been so decisively defeated and wanted $18,000,000 a great deal more than it did three virtually unexploited territorial outposts. Even so, there might have been more hemming and hawing over the treaty (March 10, 1848) if the reports coming out of California about a gold discovery, about two months earlier (January 24) had been taken seriously by anyone but a few Californians and Oregonians.

Certainly no one in eastern Mexico had had time to hear of the rumor in any important way, and no one in the eastern United States, except a few wild-eyed gamblers, did much but kid the reports till the following November when Governor (also Colonel) Richard Baker's messenger, a Lieutenant Loeser, arrived in Washington with a tea caddy (some say an oyster can—one prefers the caddy because it would have been a much more likely container for carriage) containing 234 ounces of dust sufficiently pure to be worth about $3000.

To explain why the 1848 Rush was an almost purely local affair in 1848 one has only to consider Lieutenant Loeser's course on his swift-winged flight to get the caddy from San Francisco to Washington. First he went to Paita, Peru. There he got a boat to Panama and crossed the Isthmus where he found another boat going to Jamaica. From Jamaica he was able to sail to New Orleans and from New Orleans to Washington. The trip took from August 17 to November 24, three months, and a week for this Hermes, this lightning courier. Don't laugh. It would have taken four to eight months around the Horn.

The dust was put on display in the War Office just about the time some 30,000 young Americans, our bloodiest and our best, came back from the Mexican exercise—25,000 of them in one convoy—with a strong disinclination to go back to the plow or the dry-goods counter or wherever they had been working about two years before. (We had more troops than that in the war, of course—nearer 100,000, but about 12,000 were regulars, some were killed, and slightly over 800 were already occupying California.)

A third factor which contributed in some small measure to the settlement of the Fields was the general unrest in Europe. The German states were yelling for constitutional government; Louis Philippe, the King of France, had to run to England and a republic was declared; there were riots in Austria and Italy—all of these affairs were attended by violence. Now, no matter who wins one of these arguments, someone loses and finds it prudent to travel for his health; America got an undue proportion of the fugitives, usually good stock. Good enough to have made themselves noticeable to possible hangmen. The new gold fields naturally got their share, which accounts for the number of barons and counts—a few of them genuine—who turned up around San Francisco and points east with remarkable promptness.

Aside from this European influx, the Orient sent its offering. Virtually every able-bodied young man in Hawaii arrived and this included every kind of Polynesian. The Chinese population in California grew from about 660 in 1850 to about 25,000 two years later. The Japanese did not participate, since these islands were not opened by Perry till 1853. (Treaty ratified, 1854, when the principal excitement was nearly over.)

(It may be observed that almost every statistic in this book has been or will be accompanied by the journalistic cowardice of "about." It cannot be helped; people were too busy digging to count.)

This accounts in a small degree for the polyglot, socially mangled population of the Fields. The Americans usually had a

small majority after 1849, but in some regions for some years
after that time the Latin Americans had a near parity and sometimes a small majority. A second and more reliable Federal
census of California was made in 1860 when the state with
324,000-odd had more than tripled the 1850 figures and the increase was chiefly American.

In the first nine years of production, and that would certainly
extend at least five years beyond anything resembling a "rush,"
the Fields produced about $370,000,000—Bancroft and Paul are
widely apart on their annual estimates, perhaps because one
credited the gold to the year it was probably dug and the other
to the year it was actually shipped, but they are only $3,000,000
apart—a little less—on the nine year total, which is negligible
on figures that had to be largely speculative, at best.

That is an average of $41,000,000 a year, which is a great deal
of money to most, though not all, individuals to this day; but
the Rush was not conducted by one person. In 1849 Paul estimates they shipped about $11,000,000. Old John Jacob Astor
died in 1848, the first year of the Rush, leaving an estate of
$20,000,000 accumulated by the simple method of making
drunkards out of Indians. That was, of course, in the process of
getting their furs. There were a number of millionaires in the
country at the time; there were supposed to be twelve in Philadelphia, of whom Gustavus Myers ("History of Great American Fortunes") says probably three actually had $1,000,000.
Anyone with a great deal of money was called a millionaire in
those days.

Old John Jacob could have bought out all of the '49ers almost
twice over and still have had enough money left to start the
New York Public Library as he did with $400,000—what was
then considered an incredible benevolence. And there was no
comparison between what he invested and what the miners
invested—in the one case a doubtful shrewdness or cunning and
in the other, blood, sweat, tears and lives.

For the Gold Rush was not a paying proposition in the large view. The principal writers on the enterprise consider that it cost about three times as much in labor and materials to produce an ounce of gold as the gold was worth—arbitrarily as gold, not for use, for which it is worth almost nothing except in dentistry and the arts. Perhaps in medicine.

The editor of *The London Times* said sourly, in 1850, that if California was not the richest place in the world it soon would be, accounting the wealth that went into it against the gold that came out.

Superficially, perhaps actually, that was absolutely true.

TWO

Off guard, the ordinary citizen will state that the first person to discover gold in California was Sutter; it was his millwright, John Marshall, who laid the egg that started the business. But even he was not the discoverer, any more than Columbus was the discoverer of America. Both "discoverers" merely made a big noise about it at an opportune moment. They were working gold in California for a good many years before the Rush. In 1842 they were mining for fifteen leagues on the rancho of Juan Manuel Vaca, and these works had extended to thirty leagues by 1844, but apparently the Mexicans had picked a thin spot and the best they could do was a dollar or two a day.

Governor Alvarado suggested to the home government in Mexico the advisability of surveying and developing the deposits and was told to stick to farming. This was good advice, but not the way the Mexicans farmed. About one hundred Mexicans were working in the mines in 1844, but they grew discouraged and went away. In 1842 Abel Stearns, not further identified, sent the Philadelphia mint 20 ounces (18 plus troy, approx.) on which the report was, "Before melting, 18 34-100ths oz.; fineness, .926–1000; value $344.75; deduct expenses sending to Philadelphia and agency there, $4.02; net $340.73."

By December, 1843, five or six years before the Rush, 2000 ounces had been taken from the San Fernando mines and most of it shipped to the Philadelphia mint, but it is difficult to stir up any excitement in Philadelphia over anything, let alone such an *outré* matter as a little gold from California. It is safe to say, though, without knowing its fineness, that the 2000 ounces were worth somewhere around $35,000, but since it represented the labors of a great many people over considerable time, it passed without notice. Many monasteries had been pillaged in the troubles of the Mexican Revolution, not too long before, and that amount of gold was a whisper to what had disappeared from the churches. Though ornamental gold is not usually, or ever, .926 fine.

Though John Augustus Sutter was only an instrument in the "discovery," and a very unwilling one, any story of the Rush must, of course, include him, if only as a *deus ex machina.* Also he was a most unusual and interesting person, part clown and part king, part saint and part swindler.

Sutter was born in a fair-sized town in Switzerland in 1803. He operated what James Peter Zollinger, his most substantial biographer, calls a "dry-goods store." However, various references, particularly on the businesses of his creditors, sound as if the shop went considerably beyond a draper's establishment. It makes little difference; he mishandled it into bankruptcy, realized everything he could on what he had—not "left," but on hand—because he owed for most of his stock, and ran off to America, leaving his wife and two sons to fend for themselves.

One of his apologists says that it would have done no one any good if he had stayed and gone to jail. Debt was still a jailing crime. If he had left anything for his wife the creditors would have taken it anyway, but it was shading morals a bit fine to clean up on everything loose whether he owned it or not.

Sutter was an expansive person, both genial and impressive. His first stop in America in 1834 was in St. Louis, where there were already plenty of Germans and enough of Sutter's countrymen to have created an atmosphere of *Gemütlichkeit* (which means something like friendly high spirits, active geniality) and none so *gemütlich* as John Augustus Sutter.

Here the dealer in ladies' dresses and household goods be-

came "Captain" Sutter, formerly of the Royal Swiss Guard of
Charles X of France. Since Louis Philippe had kicked Charles
off the throne some four years before, this seemed a safe, unidentifiable, military commission to hold. If any proof were
needed, one had only to look at Sutter's mustaches, magnificent
even in those days of splendid mustaches.

After two trading expeditions to Santa Fe—Sutter was able
to borrow without much trouble all his life, but he had a persistent yearning to jingle some money that he had earned himself—the man had the notion of starting up a settlement in
California. There is no doubt that he envisioned an empire from
the very first. Small operations did not interest him.

So he joined a party going to the Pacific Northwest, and, as in
the case of Lieutenant Loeser already noted, discovered that
the longest way round was the shortest way home. He took a
boat to Hawaii from the North, which occasionally sent a boat
to San Francisco, and spent the winter in the Islands, making
himself enormously popular and reaping letters of introduction
like mad. In the spring he had a chance to go to the Russian
settlement in Sitka, where he was again warmly welcomed,
and managed to scrounge the use of a schooner from the Rus-
ske, there mainly to take hides and oil. The boat took him to
San Francisco.

The scrounging began again on a grander scale in that place.
The Mexican governor, vastly impressed by the enormous
packet of introductions Sutter had now been able to obtain,
nevertheless looked a bit doubtful about a large land grant
till Sutter explained that he wanted land across the coastal
range, in the valley between those mountains and the Sierra
Nevadas. Then the governor beamed upon Sutter. For in this
year, 1839, when the Mexicans had held California for two hundred years or so—longer as a property of exploration—they had
never made the slightest settlement in this valley country, one
of the richest in the world, but filled with bad Indians, and too

remote from the routes to the homeland. But they were dubious about foreign settlement along the coast.

Alvarado gave him about fifty thousand acres (48,818) which was a mere token, because Sutter knew he could have as much as he wanted when he wanted it. So his expedition, which excited both the doubts and the mirth of the Mexican authorities set off up the river to Sutter's proposed empire. He had three Kanakas from Hawaii, one of them a female who was wife of his right-hand navigator, and became his "housekeeper," and a dozen or so "white" men whom he had picked up around the place. Also three cannon and a reasonable supply of beans and other provisions; also a large amount of Captain Sutter's luggage.

The peculiar genius of this dubious promoter, who had managed to live in considerable comfort for five or six years after escaping, bankrupt and worse, from his creditors in Switzerland, now became apparent. On the trip up the Sacramento Sutter was threatened by the "bad" Indians. They were shortly working for him at about two beads a day. First he demonstrated his cannon, harmlessly, and then he demonstrated his charm, fatally.

The long story—not so long at that, nine years—of how Sutter established his fort and became the lord of 146,454 acres, as near as makes no difference, 230 square miles, is not particularly pertinent to the story of gold in California. His dominion was not limited by his actual grant; he was the power in this outland, and though it was necessary to keep the records straight by placating the Mexicans and the Indians with a show of legality, he could have had, legally, as much as he wanted—ten times the 230 square miles if he had known what to do with them.

Comes 1848 and Sutter has his little empire, with several flour mills and, what was more important as a symbol of government, a distillery which made, apparently, plain liquor for ordinary purposes and very good liquor for Captain Sutter and his guests, and for special rewards.

It was not part of Sutter's plan, as it was Astor's, to exploit the Indians with alcohol, but he quickly learned that it was necessary to pacify the white people with that ameliorative of life. He was doing quite well till he had the notion of buying out the Russian properties north of him in California—a purchase in line with his lordly ideas, which he always managed to keep about a mile and a half ahead of his capacities, mental and financial.

His mortgages and the Gold Rush ruined him; each in part, but together irremediably. He might have paid the mortgages if there had been no "Rush," but then he would undoubtedly have gone into some other extravagance to increase his kingdom; he was insatiable in satisfying the grandeur of John Augustus Sutter, the bankrupt draper who had deserted his family in Switzerland, fifteen or sixteen years before.

The insatiability was combined with a kindliness without which none of the charm which he possessed would have been possible. Charm without such generosity and innate humanity is transparent and Sutter was admired, affectionately, almost on sight, by Americans, Latins, Indians and Kanakas. His pilot and trustiest henchman was a Kanaka whose wife he shared, apparently to the pleasure, and certainly not to the displeasure, of any of them.

During the bitterest days of the '49ers he was most industrious in sending out rescue parties for the greenhorns and unfortunates who were stranded in the Sierras—he sent two Indian guides to the famous Donner party, which, being too weak to follow the reds did the next best thing and ate them. It is not recorded that they ever thanked Captain Sutter for this refreshment. He sheltered everyone who staggered within searching distance of the Fort, supplied them, and helped them on their way. At the same time he was playing at being both American and Mexican at once to protect his tiny empire.

This is slightly ahead of the catastrophe. The aching shortage at Sutter's fort was lumber; there was very little timber in this valley of the Sacramento, and the importing of sawed material was prohibitively expensive. So he commissioned an eccentric New Jersey Scotsman, John Marshall, to build him a sawmill, in reach of timber and also of the Fort. (Incidentally, in two or three of his letters he spells Marshall's name indiscriminately, sometimes "Martial." In Gudde's edition of Sutter's diaries and notes the English is correct; in Zollinger's biography the direct transcripts are far from correct. Sutter could be eloquent in English but it was by no means his native tongue, if he had one. He was probably best in French and German.)

At any rate, Marshall rode in from the mill one evening in as great a lather as his horse and handed Sutter a small quantity of yellow dust wrapped up in a rag. After a great deal of mystery, which made Sutter, knowing the man's eccentricities, regret that he had no weapon at hand, Marshall confided that the dust was gold. After a consultation with the encyclopedia they put the stuff through two simple tests, nitric acid, and specific gravity as compared to silver, and concluded that it really was gold.

Sutter was not delighted; however, he took some comfort from the possibility that there was only a little of the stuff. His projects and economies were not founded on mining but on farming, and from the first he had a premonition of what promptly happened. So, when he rode over to the mill to reconnoiter he speaks of his "melancholy ride."

The fact was as bad as he had feared—truly, it was worse, for the workers, assuming that the "Old Cap" would be as delighted as they were by the discovery, had salted the sluices and the showing was impressive.

Sutter was appalled; he had long since asked the Indians to bring him any curiosities they found, artifacts, minerals, anything else, and "they had brought me everything but gold." It is most likely that they did not consider gold a curiosity, since they must have run upon nuggets now and then. They certainly did not value the stuff, for at the time and for years afterward they would dig all day for the white men for a few drinks of liquor or a few yards of cloth.

Sutter and Marshall had a curious crew on their hands. There were fourteen Mormons, from a party Brigham Young had sent by sea to acquire a promised land as insurance if Salt Lake City did not pan out, five others of less heterodox religions, if any, and numbers of Indians, varying from time to time as the tribesmen felt occasional needs for beads, blankets, or brandy.

All of these Sutter swore to secrecy for six weeks till the mill could be completed. Apparently these men kept the matter quiet, scrupulously, but the cook knew about it, independently or through her husband, and the cook was a woman.

A short time afterward Sutter sent a Swiss teamster up to the camp with a wagonload of provisions. "I should have sent one of the Indians," he said with a rueful implicit reference to the propensities of his countrymen for liquor and conversation.

In the kitchen the teamster, Jacob Wittmer, found one of Mrs. Weimer's or Wimmer's children (Bancroft spells it one way and Sutter another, but Sutter, as has been mentioned, also spelled "Marshall," "Martial") playing with some shiny flakes.

"See what I've got," the child said. "Gold."

The teamster laughed.

"You don't need to laugh," said the fond but gabby mother, "it really is gold."

Wittmer took her word for it and collected a little of the stuff.

Some time before, Sutter had made arrangements with two Mormons, Sam Brannan and George Smith (a relative of old Joseph, the prophet), to run a small store in one of his buildings. Among other things they sold liquor, and liquor, being irrecoverable, was cash.

So appeared Mr. Wittmer, ordered a bottle of brandy, and

offered a small sack of dirt in payment. Smith was indignant.
"You know what the rules are here—no cash, no brandy."

"That's cash," said Wittmer. "It's gold. Ask Old Cap."

With profound apologies for bringing him such a ridiculous
story, Smith did ask Sutter and Sutter regretfully told him that
it was gold. This was the worst possible place that the find could
have been advertised. Isaac Humphrey, a miner from Georgia,
had reported some time before, in San Francisco, that there was
gold along the American River, but no one believed him. A
storekeeper, however, has a hundred mouths, and all of them
are loud.

"So a drunkard and a talkative woman spread the news," Sutter said later.

Brannan was full of enterprise. He appears at various mo-
ments in the history of the Rush and of Sacramento, San
Francisco, and sometimes, incredibly, quite favorably. A gold
excitement would mean prospectors and prospectors would
mean business. It is not very likely that he realized what it
would do to Sutter.

Sam Brannan was an opportunist; one wonders a little bit
about his profession of Mormonism. It got him to the Coast,
all right. A little later, when the Rush was going full swing,
as far as California, Oregon, and Northern Mexico were concerned, Brigham Young appointed Sam to collect 30 per cent
of all gold dug by Mormons to go to the building of a temple
for the Lord in Salt Lake City.

Brannan collected it, but was strangely procrastinative about
giving up any of the moneys. Young sent a messenger with a
direct demand for the gold for the Lord's temple.

"Tell the Lord to send me a receipt," said Brannan, "and I'll
send it at once."

He was a long way from the Destroying Angels, etc., and
after that was considered more or less a gentile.

Brannan believed in direct methods, so he simply got a pouch

or two of gold, mounted his horse and rode up and down the
streets of San Francisco yelling, "Gold! Gold! Gold on the
American River!"

For some reason, perhaps partly because of the previous visit
of Isaac Humphrey, but more probably because of Sam's
method of announcement, the San Franciscans dropped whatever they were doing and rushed for Sacramento.

The bell was tolling for Sutter, but at first it seemed that it
might be a mere clamor of celebration. He owned all the cattle, all the grain, every facility along the American River and
when the gold really appeared he had a brief harvest. He pros-
pered enormously, but only for weeks or a few months. Then
the newcomers began to take rather than buy; they stole his
cattle, they trampled his grain fields, which he could not have
harvested, anyway, for want of labor, they stole all the lumber
of his sawmill—so thoroughly that it was afterward somewhat
difficult to find its precise location—they abused his hospitality
at the same time they planned raids on his lands. They even
stole three mill wheels, probably as bases on which to mash
quartz.

At this moment of disaster the Russians descended on him.
He had obviously been "slow pay" on his debts all his life and
they seized this moment of opportunity to demand their ar-
rears on the payments for some land he had never needed, a
scant supply of poor animals, a lot of broken tools and some
rotten harness.

Sutter had sent for his Swiss family at just about the beginning of the gold outbreak and he now attempted to meet the
Russian obligation with some silly evasion of deeding the purchase to his son. (They did not jail debtors in America at this
time.)

But it was all over. Sutter moved East a little while later to
bring claims for restitution before Congress, but because of his
Mexican citizenship and land titles the thing became as con-

fused as Jarndyce vs. Jarndyce. California gave him a small
pension finally, and he retired eventually to a little place in
Pennsylvania called Lititz, where he petitioned Congress and
wrote memoirs for thirty years or so till he died in 1880. The
last of the first of the barons of California.

THREE

Sutter had sense enough to attempt to conceal his discovery till he could consolidate his position. Except for Sam Brannan he might have come through the business extremely well. With a little preparation he could have summoned his small army and thrown out the invaders or buried them whenever they trespassed. He was caught in unfortunate circumstances; he was a Mexican magistrate but as a resident of America, and apparently never a citizen, it was doubtful if he was even a landowner. What might have been execution at one moment in 1848, might have been murder a few months later, after California had become part of the United States.

The position of the Mormons on the whole business was rather admirable—after the 30-per-cent episode with Brannan they simply pulled out. Some of them, of course, succumbed to the Calf of Gold and abandoned Joseph Smith's tablets of gold; but most of them acceded to Brigham Young's command for them to come to the new home in Salt Lake City.

Brigham said:

"The true use of gold is for paving streets, covering houses and making culinary dishes; and, when the saints shall have preached the gospel, raised grain and built up cities enough, the Lord will open up the way for a supply of gold to the perfect satisfaction of His people. Until then, let them not be over-anxious, for the treasures of the earth are in the Lord's storehouse, and he will open the doors thereof when and where he pleases."

Gold would not be very satisfactory for paving, though as the decoration for roofs it is used on a good many public buildings; but the program was sound at the moment for the Mormons, who were much more in need of tillage than they were of dross. On the average, people who tended their cabbages, Mormon or gentile, did much better than the people who rushed for gold.

The Californians were not as wise as Sutter. They went to great lengths to advertise their good fortune in the East—to such lengths that the East disregarded the whole business. It was generally supposed to be merely a hysteria or else a device to get immigrants.

"The streams are paved with gold," said the alcalde of San Francisco, "—the mountains swell in their golden girdles—it sparkles in the sands of the valleys—it glitters in the coronets of steep cliffs."

The editor of the New York *Literary American* said, "The author may have thought there was poetry in this, but he knew, as well as we do, that there was no truth in it."

But before he was through with his piece he cautiously admitted that there might be something to the rumors. Public prints, with their thousands of potential critics, are forced to concessions that no barroom would tolerate a minute.

As was mentioned, what made believers in the East was, first, that unrebuttable tea caddy (or oyster can) of gold, but finally President Polk's statement in his message of December 5, about two weeks after Loeser's arrival, that gold had been found in California, put the cap on the business. Overnight, the East went up with a splendid Whoosh!

Not only the East, but the South and the new Midwest. However, the East was best prepared to move instantly, because of its shipping. It was like that night in 1938 when the Martians invaded New Jersey—and the drops of a dozen New Jersey telephone switchboards near the site of the invasion fell with magnificent unanimity. So it was in the harbors and docks of the Eastern seaboard.

Everything for the Horn was booked instantly and every possible boat was taken off its ordinary routes and routed for San Francisco, willy-nilly. Old hulks fit for nothing but a little coastal trading and older ones fit only for breaking up were suddenly hauled out, patched up, and advertised as elegant accommodations to San Francisco. Whatever the Rush did for the miners, it was pure gold for the shipyards and mushroom transportation companies all along the Atlantic coast. Any scow that could get far enough away from Newport or Bath or Boston or Philadelphia not to attract attention when it sank, was tacked together and booked to the top of its mizzenmast as soon as it had advertised its intention of going to California.

Oddly enough, not too many of these miserable derelicts seem to have sunk on the dangerous passages around Hatteras or later at the Horn itself. They apparently sailed by and large, for one account mentions that in approaching the equator the boat was a good deal nearer Africa than South America. The graveyard seems to have been between San Francisco and Peru, going both ways, and many wrecks were occasioned by hugging the land too closely in order to save mileage—and use winds.

Press and pulpit—an odd old phrase, since each institution spends a lot of hopeless time trying to make peace with the other—thundered (or whiffled) against the hysteria or fever. After the sermon or editorial the preacher, or editor, booked passage for San Francisco, the one to educate the miners, and the other to save their souls. Absent-mindedly, they put shovels in their luggage.

The seafarers were not as limited in luggage as the later overlanders. Even a small boat can carry a great deal more than a covered wagon and these people loaded up generously with every nonsensical bit of equipment that could be suggested by the carrion crows who spread their goods in the newspapers, the brief periodicals designed for the adventurers, and the multitude of handbooks on How to Get to California and How to Dig Gold. "How To's" we have always with us.

They took out dredges, ore mills—some report must have come back about quartz mining—patent machines for extracting gold by heat or chemistry, and even diving suits to search the bottoms of the deeper rivers and creeks. Tents and sleeping bags and tarpaulins—every kind of camp equipment and clothing and utensil; superior hardware, picks, shovels, sledges, Colt revolvers—these had just had a good testing in the Mexican War—knives, axes, provisions of all kinds.

Half of this stuff littered the beaches of San Francisco till it was slowly dispersed by rust and plundering for parts, or by being shoved out of the way into the bay. "If we had known what was needed," Franklin Buck (q.v., later) mourned, "we could have made a fortune." He was already loaded with flour and provisions, and a big shipment had just arrived from Chile.

The trouble of not knowing what was needed was very common. At one time a small cookstove, worth about $8.00 in the East, cost one miner 10 ounces ($170). At another a whole cargo of unwanted stoves was used to patch a mudhole in a San Francisco street.

The firstcomers out were the fortunate ones. On seaworthy ships they made the turn of the Horn, and most of them, with old New England whaling pilots, could cut off a little mileage by going through the very roughly charted straits of Magellan above the Horn, north of Tierra del Fuego. They might save some time that way or they might not. Buck mentions that, after achieving this perilous passage, his boat was driven back below 59 degrees latitude, which was about midway between the South Pole and San Francisco. The ships that really turned the Horn might have left messages with the penguins to deliver to Shackleton and Amundsen a little later.

The route was slower than Panama, but actually slower by only a few weeks at best, as ship communications were then. One might lose those weeks waiting for a boat in Panama City, after rather horrible discomforts and disease on the Isthmus.

But for the westerners, who were already more than a thousand miles on their way to the Fields, the business of traveling back to the eastern seaboard, away from the coasts of California, in order to embark on a slow voyage by a circuitous route to a place already a thousand miles nearer, seemed a geographical consideration beyond any argument.

There was also the question of expense. Aside from the cost of traveling that far, before embarking, there was the cost of passage. The prices were various—anywhere from $300 to $1200. No one very far west of the Atlantic had much cash. They did not need a great deal because the few pieces of currency that got into the western settlement were sufficient for a people who traded grain for flour, hides for shoes, and logs for lumber, when they did not saw the boards themselves. Still, they desired a few things from the East, not by necessity, but by preference.

So the first solid immigration was accomplished by Yankees rather than westerners. ("Yankee" is still a doubtful word, though it seems most probably to have derived from Scotch "yankie," sharp, or clever. The Dutch idea of "Jan Kees"—an ordinary person—seems not pertinent, since the Dutch were not important when the term became common as representing all definable Americans.)

The best reference on this business is the short account of the New England trader, Buck mentioned, a merchant's man out of New York from New England, who escorted some of his employers' goods from New York to San Francisco. His book is *Yankee Trader in the Gold Rush*. It was a pleasant trip, replete with backgammon boards, wine, and a library of two hundred fifty volumes.

The child—he was about twenty-one—messed everything up, as might have been expected. He managed to get in a good deal of practice on his flute and he wrote to his sister regularly, insisting that he was not drinking to excess and that he was not engaged to any of the girls back home. Aside from a short note of approval on Rio de Janeiro, his letters fall considerably short of Baedeker, but one has the impression of an easy pleasant journey.

Buck's captain must have done his best at northing by tacking toward the west, and he finally reached the latitude of San Francisco with twelve hundred miles of longitude to walk. Buck does not say what he did in this strait; he probably tacked on the north to make east.

Young Buck's log, violently condensed and interpreted, was as follows:

Leave N.Y. Jan. 18, 1849. Girls send flowers and "Bachelor's Friends" (sewing packets) possibly with eye to remote possibility of returning millionaires.

Arrive Rio, March 11, 52 days. Pretty girls rife.

The Cape. Capt. did Magellan's Strait above Tierra but wind blew them back to 59 degrees—plus after passage. No girls.

Callao, May 31. Girls not much.

Lima, nice cathedral, altar said to be silver, but might be tin or pewter. Most beautiful women yet observed. Place for return, especially since I do not want a lock of ——'s hair or all the hair she has.

San Francisco, Aug. 6. No girls at all.

Buck puts his sailing time down at 180 days, so he must have deducted the stopovers. Buck's sister somehow got the idea by some suggestion in his messages that what he most needed was the love of a good woman, and worked at it. He was finally trapped, but many years later, on a trip back to New England, by a girl named Jenny. Buck had far more interest in music than in mining. In spite of his 175 hard pounds and nearly six

feet of height, he declared himself out as far as digging was concerned, and set himself to a complicated system of trading. He
went to the mines once, in desperation, and dug $100 in five
months. Even with bad luck this was hardly possible if one used
a shovel regularly. Gold is hard to dig with a flute.

As Buck made it, though he never made much else in his
life but five children and a dairy farm, the idea was strictly to
make as much money as possible without doing any work. His
experience of trading made each of his trading posts successful but never quite as successful as the next one might be, so
he escaped a fortune and complained regularly in his letters to
his sister about his LUCK. (His caps.) Jenny finally pinned him
down to milking Jersey cattle on a little California rancho and
they apparently lived quite comfortably the rest of their lives.

One of the lad's observations on the Pacific Ocean should be
framed in gold at Phillips Andover, where he had his education.
"I sometimes think that the greater part of the earth's surface
must be covered by water."

Another observation, more to the point, is that San Francisco
had a population of about 5000 when he arrived in August,
1848, and about 20,000 when he left, in October, for more trade
nearer the Fields.

Though flour was selling for $7.00 when he arrived with a
lot of it—the low price was caused by recent Chilean imports
—he dispensed with his cargo and later bought it at $18 to sell
at $44 up at his store in Sacramento. This gave him a fair profit,
in spite of freighting, which cost $7.50 a hundred.

Not everyone who rounded the Horn feasted on pheasant
and wine on the Fourth of July or whiled the idle hours away
at backgammon or with one of the two hundred fifty books in
the ship's library. This was a voyage de luxe, planned by a
trader for a trader. In spite of the fact that "Uncle Richard"
chose a blithering idiot to manage the commercial side of the
affair, he broke even or somewhat better on account of four pre-

fabricated houses which were sent to accommodate the traders. These sold for $4000 each. Buck took $2800 as his share of the profits, but he had to pay $1.50 for a can in which to store his dust.

On the whole, however, the first seafarers had it easy, even in the rotten craft in which many of them put to sea. New Englanders had been sailing around the Horn, in the China trade, or whaling, for about two centuries and they knew the way and what was required to follow it. The hardships occurred later when the boats were terribly overloaded. The coffee was excellent and plentiful, since they broke their trip at Rio, but the live meat, hogs and chickens, gave out somewhere toward Callao and the regular stew of salt pork and beans became tiresome.

New England went wild, if not in direct action toward the Fields, in the vicarious participation of the "companies." If one could not go himself he could at least buy a share in a miner or party that *was* going. The parties were financed—sometimes they even had their own ships built—prepared by many councils, and indoctrinated.

A ribald writer, undoubtedly a liar, speaks of his preparation:

"The preacher addressed us and he said, 'Young men, you are going to California with the Bible in one hand and New England culture in the other. It is your duty to spread these things through the new land.'

"Then the most eminent citizen, father of one of the boys who was going, addressed us and concluded, 'Young men, you are going to California with the Bible in one hand and New England culture in the other. It is your duty to spread these things through the new land.'

"Then a message was read, from President Everett of Harvard: 'Young men you are going to California with a Bible in one hand, etc.'"

This gave them a cargo of three Bibles each, and that was none too many. For it is probably not a lie that a little later one of the pilgrims tossed in a Bible on a trade with an Indian who needed paper for rifle wadding. The deal was noted by several people and approved, as were all swindles on the Indians.

The companies were generally far more sanguine than the individuals, their enthusiasms being multiplied by the numbers of their members. (Cf., Le Bon and Everett Dean Martin on *The Mob.*) The Hartford Union Mining and Trading Company made a provision in its contracts that if so much gold was stored as to endanger their boats, one of which was building, the surplus was to be kept under tarpaulins, with guards, till other boats were available. Tarpaulins for gold.

Another company, even more bedimmed, provided that the miners should report in San Francisco with their booty every evening. Sacramento was about one hundred fifty miles from San Francisco by the river and no one could hope to make the round trip in less than a week. The fare at some moment in 1850 mentioned by Bancroft was $250 for the round trip, $150 one way.

The realities promptly broke up the companies. Mining was a one- or two-man business, three or four at the most. Anyway, the obligations of New England rested lightly on the miners of California—a long way off. The companies were as if they had never been. A few of the patrons were paid off, but not many. There is still a trace of conscience in New Englanders, and, with a Bible in one hand and New England culture in the other, the miners paid off possibly 1 per cent of their debts, told everyone to go to hell, and kept on digging on their own.

As the ships came in the whole place became a dissentious, quarreling cosmopolis. The Georgians, the Germans, and the Welsh were respected because they knew something about mining. The French huddled together and made no slightest effort to accommodate themselves to the language and customs of the barbaric races.

The French were known as "Keskadees" which is a fair translation of "What is that of the what he has said." They were neither liked nor disliked. The Germans, called "Dutch," mingled immediately. They learned English as easily as the Americans came to understand some German—at least, in phrases, because of the kindred Saxon vocabularies.

It is obvious that these first adventurers must have been the cream or scum of eastern youth, because they had the money to pay passage on the one hand, and nothing much else to do on the other; that is, no prospect that was more important than the big gamble, but some substance. Whatever leavening the original ferment of California had must have come from these long-nosed Yankees. They were, finally, blessed in their project by the Church and the magistrates; it was no such unloading of undesirables as Italy and Ireland practiced on America a little later, and England on Australia and New Zealand, and France on French Guiana and Morocco.

These boys had to have $300 and another $300 in equipment, very considerable sums at the time, or they couldn't go. So they were not paupers or refugees.

Their proportion of success was naturally far higher than that of the vagrants who came in a little later. But some of this proportion can be attributed to the fact that a good many of them had sense enough to start boarding houses, or to buy potatoes from Chile on the low market and sell them later for their weight in dust. The distressing frictions of a shovel never blistered their lily fingers.

In the first year a few dozen millionaires—that is, people who had managed to make $20,000 or more—left the mines forever and returned to the lush granite of New England, or the rich soil of the South and Midwest, to become squires. That is one of the things that makes statistics difficult. One does not only neglect to remark failures but the successes are like the farmer's tenth pig. ("I have nine pigs and another one who ran around so fast I couldn't count him.") I don't suppose my grandfather was ever counted. He hit the Field early in 1850, sent gold back to Iowa by various means of transport, including his own pockets, and left in 1852, carrying a good deal of dust directly to the Philadelphia mint. That this was ever recorded as mining or population is very doubtful, though it is probably recorded in the mint records.

The real strike of the '49ers was not made by the men with picks and shovels. They furnished the fuel, but the flame came from the suppliers. Twenty people made fortunes at the expense of one digger who starved.

Many New Englanders came in in their normal capacity as traders. When gold was brought to stores in San Francisco or Sacramento, why pursue it further?

As will be increasingly apparent, the men who went out to California to work and make a small, adequate insurance for their futures at farming or shopkeeping, or whatever their stars indicated, usually succeeded. The almost unanimous majority, who planned to pick up a few lumps of gold and get drunk, did not succeed. Except in the latter aim.

FOUR

There were a number of transcontinental routes—across country, across Mexico, across Nicaragua, and also by air. This last modus did not work, though it was promoted by no less a person than the editor of *Scientific American,* a periodical which I read devoutly every month now that it has sobered up.

Mr. Rufus Porter, the editor at the time, designed a balloon and offered passage for only $200—a two-day trip at 100 miles an hour. The vessel was to be built of spruce rods—balsa had not been discovered—covered with 8000 yards of waterproofed cloth. This cloth, filled with hydrogen, was supposed to support 300 passengers and 7 tons of machinery. It had steam engines to propel it when winds were not favorable, and lengths of copper cable to ground any lightning it might encounter.

Filled with reservations, at $50 for the Grand Trial Trip, the project was abandoned when some Philistine happened to mention air resistance to the learned editor. Mr. Porter had figured everything out very carefully but had not observed the fact that a balloon must float in some medium and that even air, that tenuous liquid, achieves some solidity when it is compressed against 100 miles an hour.

The outcome of the whole business was a mildly amusing cartoon by Mr. Currier, an engraver of the time, later to become famous with a partner named Ives, in which the balloon is pictured as departing with a large sign on its side,

PASSAGE $125 AND FOUND
(If Lost)

Probably the most favored route in this shift of population was by Panama. Reaching the Pacific was the trip almost accomplished. They thought. It was never considered, apparently, that the real enemy of the voyager was not accident, Indians, or starvation, but simply disease. They had yellow fever, malaria, dysentery, scurvy, and various unidentifiable fevers. Cholera was the greatest pest—it was carried from the eastern sea ports and New Orleans, rejoined some of its relatives in Chagres and Panama City, and had a family reunion with the Chinese and Kanakas on the gold shore.

In the heart of what considers itself the orange capital of the world—men died of scurvy and the accompanying diarrhea. Also the suicide rate of these gallant prospectors was appalling; people simply became disgusted with themselves and everything. This, after the British had fed their sailors, "limeys," fresh lime juice for a hundred years. It is true that vitamins were not to be discovered for more than sixty years, but someone should have noticed the British Navy instead of making a sour—very sour—joke about limeys.

In J. E. Sherwood's excellent *Pocket Guide to California,* one of a flood of such books that accompanied the Rush, but distinguished for being more or less practical and accurate, there is a specific instruction about the crossing of Panama. Be sure to sleep under shelter in your boat on the trip across the Isthmus. Pay no attention to the mosquitoes, they merely sting, but if the night air gets you, you are very likely to come down with fever.

Pathology had attained this wisdom in the time of our grandfathers. After several thousand Frenchmen had died of various fevers in an attempt to build a canal across the Isthmus, the Americans exterminated the little winged hypodermic needles and made a canal which would have been sheer bliss for the venturers of 1848 and '49. I once spent two or three weeks in Panama, occasionally crossing and recrossing my grandfather's trail of 1849, without seeing, hearing or feeling a mosquito and without any fever except the $6.00 I spent on the lottery. (No LUCK.)

The little village of Chagres, at the Atlantic mouth of the river of that name, was suddenly overwhelmed by such traffic as it had never dreamed was in the outside world. Chagres itself has now been overwhelmed by Colon, at the Atlantic entrance to the Panama Canal.

That is now a dying city too, since the transfer to Panama City has become a simple matter of an hour's drive and since a very elegant hotel has been built to welcome arrivals and departures, which take in most of the tourist trade. This is a pity, too, since Colon is much the more interesting town. Colon is far less expensive and much more viewable. The place has an excellent but unostentatious hotel run by the United States Government; however, I believe that it was in Balboa, on the Panama City side, that someone remarked to me about some other government hotel, "This place would have fallen down years ago except that the termites have plenty and they are in the basement making love."

When the '49ers reached the country it was simply a jungle and a morass. The Spaniards had thrown a "Royal Road" of stone across it, but Panama could digest a road, with mud and jungle, in a very few years. Nevertheless, a good many sections of the Royal Road can still be seen, and why the gold hunters did not repair it and have two or three days of safe walking across the Isthmus, instead of days of torment, would be inexplicable if one did not realize that they were in a great hurry. A good road gang, and there were plenty of laborers, could have made a viable highway across North America in a month or so. But everyone was in a hurry. So the exodus wasted a great deal of time, because there was no planning or concerted effort—for whom? Not for themselves, for the crazy Yankees. So they picked another mango, the most delicious fruit, or a bunch of bananas, which were practically in public domain, and picked up what they could from this inflatus of lunatics. The longer they were visited the more they gained.

Panama still has a law that foreigners cannot own land in the country, which has made it somewhat impoverished but extremely agreeable.

On the eastern seaboard of the United States shipowners were immediately able to route boats to this dangerous bit of swamp and hills. My grandfather, living on an American adventure in Iowa, had to go to New Orleans and then to Havana to get shipping to Panama. One can now drive across the American continent in about an hour, from Panama City to Colon, or vice versa, but at that time, with paddling up the Chagres River and walking over a trail that had been churned hip-deep in mud, the traverse took two or three days.

At the Pacific end there was—nothing. There were a few government boats around, principally because of the recent acquisition of California and some troubles with England over the territorial boundaries of Oregon, but, in spite of the fact that boats took on three hundred passengers in accommodations designed for a third or a sixth of that number, there was a jam at Panama City. The rage to reach the mines was such that several companies bought rowboats to coast up to San Francisco. They were never heard of again.

The newly formed Pacific Mail Steamship Line had five boats running to Chagres and three boats going as far as Astoria on the Pacific side, but they hardly took a drop from the bucket. The *California,* which was designed to crowd in as many as one hundred passengers, booked four hundred in January, 1849, and contemporaries say there were at least five hundred aboard. In February, 1849, sixty ships left New York for Panama, seventy left Philadelphia and Boston, eleven left New Bedford; Bancroft thinks that these boats averaged about fifty passengers each, for California. This would come to about seven

thousand people in this month, of whom not more than one
thousand could be carried from Panama to San Francisco during the next month or so.

Naturally this state of affairs did not last long, or Panama
City would be the biggest town in the world. As soon as China
clippers and various craft could be rerouted, in these days before cables and radio, they were sent to pick up the pilgrims.
Which causes the reflection that if Panama had built a railroad
across the strait, as Vanderbilt did across Nicaragua a few years
later, there would have been no particular incentive to build
a canal, and Colon and Panama City might now be two of the
great cities of the world at the termini of transoceanic railroad
trade. Oh, probably the Yankees would have wrecked things by
building the Canal anyway.

The Yankees naturally took over Panama City but they seem
to have done it in a quite good-humored and unobjectionable
fashion. One policeman was killed during the winter and a few
houses were burned now and then in celebrations, but since
the houses could be rebuilt with a few banana trees and the
Panamanians have never regarded policemen, of any brief re-
gime, as essential to their happiness, the races got along very
well, considering the pressure. It must be remembered, too,
that the Panamanians were growing rich on this traffic, without the bother of going to California.

FIVE

There are several reasons, as were suggested, why the overland routes took most of the miners to the gold fields. In the first place, anyone living in Kentucky, Missouri, Iowa or Illinois, anywhere in the Ohio-Mississippi-Missouri basin, had already taken a long hop toward the Field; in the second place, anyone who had established residence in such a remote place as the Midwest had not done it to take piano lessons. Finally, it was the poor man's route; it did not take cash, which was conspicuously absent in the Midwest at this and most other times, world without end, Amen.

Anyone with a good span of oxen and a barrel of cured pork —and, preferably, with a fair eye for sighting a rifle—could join a company without further resources, except the understood qualification of a strong back. A feeble brain apparently did not hurt, either, for the preparations of many of these companies approached the lunatic.

One could follow the river valleys from anywhere in the eastern or southern Midwest to Independence, Missouri, the great point of departure, or St. Joseph or Council Bluffs, and resume the journey on the Platte River Valley. From here it was a little over 2000 miles to Sutter's fort. There would be a trifle of trouble beyond Salt Lake City, of course, with a bit of desert, but then they would reach the Humboldt and travel to the Sierras like a ding-dang. The Sierras were riddled with passes and, beyond that, one filled his buckets and washtubs with gold and returned to Iowa or Missouri to astound the neighbors.

Everything that could possibly happen to these enterprising pilgrims happened to them. They did not have the little mosquitoes of Panama but they had cholera and plenty of it. They had the usual dysentery, mentioned before, lots of malaria from the southern visitors who joined them at Independence and, by their community, endemics of everything that anyone could invent.

At a crossing of the Humboldt River, then unseasonably in flood as a display of God's grace, twelve people drowned themselves in one day. By choice. It was the end of the rope. The gold might be there at the end of some rainbow, but it could not possibly justify the bitterness of the existence they had suffered. They were simply not prepared for the adventure that offered itself. We are fairly smug in America nowadays—there hasn't been an endemic of cholera for more than fifty years, and yellow fever has gone with the wind.

It is mentioned in Webster or Gould that after regurgitating feces for a few days people have been known to strangle themselves with their hands. It got to be just about that bad on parts of the western trip. Though this is not the general story, of course. Most of them pushed through, but they left a dire percentage of fatalities all the way from Council Bluffs to Salt Lake City and from there to the Sierras.

There is one reasonably gruesome story, without confirmation except by the circumstantial evidence, of a fellow who was dropped to die in the Utah desert—he was infected and his friends wanted no more to do with him. Not to care for him, not to bury him—just to get away from the poisonous body that was still dangerous because it was living. He was found and lived. Others did not.

The endemic of cholera and such afflictions among the travelers is more comprehensible when one considers that for a year or two there was an almost continuous train of wagons moving along the Platte, from the Missouri to the neighborhood of Salt

Lake City, and leaving a deadly trail of excreta in every brook, river, swamp, and mudhole that it passed, for 1700 miles. The trail had become a great sewer, and not a sanitary one.

The Indian difficulties have been vastly overwritten. An incompetent named Custer—last in his class at West Point and no ornament to the U. S. Army in spite of his legends—stirred up the Sioux, but not till much later. He marched 264 American troops into an obvious trap and that made him history of sorts.

He was about the caliber of John Frémont. At the time of the '49ers, however, the Sioux were reasonably peaceful. All the Indians were horse and cattle thieves, of course, in the face of the fact that their whole living place was being stolen from them in a major operation; but they were not too aggressive about the matter. The usual overlanders crossed Sioux territory briefly between Independence and the Caddoan country of the Pawnees. Then they went on into Ute territory—the Utes, Caddoans, and Sioux understood each other about as well as I understand Hebrew, Greek, and Chinese—they were completely different people—and came to rest in a little mess of Californian Indians who could sometimes understand each other by signs. There are a dozen tribes of them, belonging to the Aztecs, the Mongolians, the Esquimaux Stems and anyone else, even if these terms are not sometimes inclusive.

The Indians actually gave the '49ers little more than some slight annoyance. The hideous atrocity of the Rush was achieved by the Mormons, the Great Meadows Massacre, where 120 gentiles or so were murdered by some of these people who believed in disappearing gold tablets. Mark Twain has taken care of them in his usual competent manner.

There have been so many stories of the excesses of human beings in their extremities that it is probably in bad taste to repeat the troubles of the Donner party. Buck's story (*Yankee Trader in the Gold Rush*), which has been mentioned, tells of his participation in a *haut-monde* tea party somewhere around

Marysville where the hostesses were two ladies who had crossed the Sierras in 1846 in the Donner party. In the absence of tea cakes these two ladies, on the crossing of the Sierras, had been compelled to eat some of their friends and companions.

In April, 1846, the Donner outfit started out from Independence in good time to make the Sierra passes before the winter. There were a hundred in the party, from Ohio, Missouri, Iowa, Illinois, and Tennessee; they picked up some casuals in Independence, and Dunbar (*History of Travel in America*) says that the procession, leaving Independence, had two hundred wagons and a thousand livestock, and stretched two miles across the plains.

This was *before* the Gold Rush. These were people simply fleeing from the civilization which had not entertained them— to California, to Oregon, anywhere away from their old failures to plan new ones. At Salt Lake City thirteen members of the party elected to follow the recommended trail north of the lake —they arrived in California a little later without any particular difficulties. The other eighty-seven took the route south of the lake, lost their way, and were caught in the mountains in October.

This party had been on the trail for months. On this desperate enterprise the fools brought along young children, babies, got their wives pregnant, carried their grandpaps and grandmas and generally behaved like the ignorant, irresponsible idiots they were. From December 17, 1846, to February of the next year the diary of Patrick Breen is a simple list of casualties.

February 26—Mrs. Murphy said here yesterday that she thought she would Commence on Milton and eat him. I do not think she has done so yet; it is distressing.

Except for the two Indian guides sent by Sutter, there is no evidence that anyone was *murdered* to feed the others. They were dying more or less naturally, sometimes at the rate of four or five a day. One man, dying, made his wife swear that she would eat her share of his body and see that their children got theirs. Finally, about Christmas, fifteen of the stronger members of the party set out to find help. Why they had waited so long is something of a mystery. Seven of them, five men and two women got through and the Californians pushed through the snow and rescued forty-odd survivors, in March, 1847.

Their curious menu was never held against the fortunate ones, except for one fellow who salted down some friends. The two ladies Buck encountered at Marysville were the social leaders of the city—partly, of course, because of their early arrival in California but chiefly because they had actually eaten a man—a feat which a great many ladies attempt but which few achieve—physically.

Two years later when Sherwood wrote his excellent *Handbook* he was particularly emphatic about innovations in routing. Stay north of Salt Lake—as most of Donner's party did not —and follow the "old" route. "This road is the best that has yet been discovered, and to the Bay of San Francisco and the Gold Region it is much the shortest. From our information we would most earnestly advise all immigrants to take this trail, without deviation, if they would avoid the fatal calamities which almost invariably have attended those who have undertaken to explore new routes."

Did Sherwood's readers do it? They did not. Rumors of short cuts were rife all the way from Missouri to the Sierras and the usual percentage of suckers—say about 90 per cent—tried one or two of them, to save forty miles here or there. Some of them lost a few days of wandering and some of them lost forty years of their lives.

Sherwood's route prescribes 2071 miles from Independence to Sutter's fort and an additional two hundred to San Francisco Bay; probably the trip ended for most of the parties at Sacramento, which was convenient to the mines. At Sherwood's estimated fifteen miles a day (by wagon) this would make a trip of very nearly five months. The fifteen miles a day is apparently conservative and makes allowance for a reasonable number of delays. The diary of Stanislaus Lasselle, of Logansport, Indiana, mentions a good many days when his party made from twenty to thirty miles on the Santa Fe route. It also mentions days when they made from five to nothing.

This Lasselle diary is vastly lightened by the capers of the Knickerbockers, a party of New Yorkers who joined the train down in Arkansas, near Fort Smith, along with natives of various other states. Mr. Lasselle did not like the New Yorkers; he did not like the southerners either, but he was comparatively tolerant of them. The Knickerbockers, however, could do no good.

April 28 (April, 1849). A Knickerbocker washing in the creek. He was boiling all the color out of his shirt. (There had to be something wrong for Mr. L. in anything a K did, even washing.)

Sunday 29. (Buffalo chase)—The Knickerbockers in the chase had double-barrel shotguns, which created a good deal of laughter and sport to the rest of the company.

Wednesday 2d. The company killed a buffalo near the train. The Knickerbockers opened it to get the heart and liver. They got the heart but could not find the liver—.

Monday 7th (May). A bear and cub killed by Dale and Buchanan. A Knickerbocker shot at the bear after it was dead—.

Tuesday 8th. A Knickerbocker knocked off his horse by fighting two others. Stuned. (Satisfaction simply reeks out of that "stuned.")

Thursday 10th. About sundown we had a terrible hail storm and strong wind blowing down some of the tents of the Knick-

erbockers. After the storm two or three of the K's crawled out
of their tents to the sport of the company.

Friday 11. A Knickerbocker kicked by a mule. He was walking leisurely along with a green veil over his face to keep the
gnats from biting him, and happening to get too close to the
mule's heels, the mule lambed away and struck him on the shin
bone. It was a severe kick, much worse than a knat bit. Several of the K's today have their faces tied up with eyes so
swollen that they as some say cannot see ten feet. What accounts for the mule kicking. A K thought that jurk meat was
so called because it was jurked off the skeleton.

(A dollar to a dime that Mr. Lasselle did not know what
"jerky" meant himself. It is from Peruvian *charqui,* via Mexico,
meaning dried meat.)

Saturday 12. A fight between two Knickerbockers. A Knickerbocker lost his coat.

Sunday 20th. A Knickerbocker took a young jack the Mexicans had packing for a young buffalo which was considered a
good joke and created a good deal of laughter.

Tuesday 22d. Some of the Knickerbockers entirely out of provisions.

Tuesday 29. Many of the Knickerbockers preparing to pack.
(That is, go home. They were camped in "Santa Fee" at the
moment.)

He drops the Knickerbockers for two months because at this
stage of the trip the train was much worried about the Apaches.
Then he reports that the K's have divided and one K is said
to have divided from his wife. Only a K would do that. After
that he lets the K's alone—the party was now about to enter
California and on August 14 the Logansport boy actually saw
gold. Nothing more from him.

This is interesting principally as it shows the violent provincialism of Americans before any extensive use of telephones, telegraphs, and railroads. They had the two latter at the time, of course, but in very limited service and only in the East. Naturally regionalism has died out completely with swift communications. In my time we in Iowa do not care whether a man comes from Boston or Cleveland, the damn easterner.

This was the southern route which seems not to have been too oppressive, except for K's, and occasional warlike Indians. The northern Indians apparently were very friendly except on occasions when they were annoyed by having their teeth kicked in. They stole, of course, but their general notion was that the Americans were crazy and would not reach where they were going, if they knew where, so it was better to put their mules and oxen to some useful purpose for the benefit of people who knew exactly where they were going. Nowhere.

They were sufficiently comfortable where they were, in violent contrast to these white people whose ancestors had traveled a tenth of the way around the world to find a good camp site, and who were traveling another tenth because their ancestors' choice had apparently not suited them. The Indians are called nomads; by choice, they never traveled a hundred miles in a generation from a spot that they had found "wa"— the Algonkian particle that means "good." Except for a slight tendency to steal horses, women, and children, which they needed, even the Sioux were commendable citizens. The Iroquois and the eastern Indians are a different kettle of fish— they seemed to have had some medieval decadences. Perhaps, as a highly socialized race, they had reached a standard of cruelty and general orneriness, *autos da fé* and crude imitations of European culture that occurred to them intuitively rather than by information from more ingenious Christians.

The number of American families that were taken on these pilgrimages seems to indicate that the average citizen, east of the Missouri, had no real conception of geography or the difficulties of the traverse. The northern route was littered with detritus, including the skeletons of people and cattle, no longer useful to the immigrants. There is a curious paradox about this abandonment; apparently this long stretch of wagons was manned by people who were essentially kindly, because there are dozens of accounts of trains which stopped to assist less fortunate parties, to pick up members and share dangerously limited supplies, to make really perilous efforts to succor others on this long and dangerous procession over distances and difficulties unsuspected at the beginning of the expedition.

And yet, when they were compelled to abandon supplies, some of them made an attempt to see that the deserted freight would be of no use to following parties. A barrel of flour would be mixed with sand and urine; a can of sugar would be doused with turpentine; a saw would be broken and hammered; a good rifle would have its barrel bent over a wagon wheel; the wheel itself would have its spokes sledged out; a dead ox would be sprinkled with strychnine, and so on—an ax would be broken over a rock, a bolt of canvas or gingham burned. The most curious thing is that the people seemed to have carried few artisans. Perhaps the artisans were doing well enough at home, but one reads, time after time, the stories of people with soleless boots or no boots at all, with tattered clothing, without ropes or cord, and so on, and this in the richest leather country in the world.

That an oxhide, let alone a buffalo hide—a few pounds of salt and a few days in the sun would have furnished all the fabric necessary to take them to China—seems to have been neglected. That they ever made use of such resources, as the settlers had made use of the deer, from Missouri to Minnesota ten or twelve years before, is not mentioned in any of a hundred or so references to the journey which one is likely to meet in the most casual reading.

They carried blacksmiths, or wheelwrights—overlapping oc-

cupations when not actually identical—most women in the
parties knew how to spin and knit, but there was no wool or
cotton. There was an endless supply of buffalo and they were
leaving dead oxen all over the place from the Platte to Sacramento.

The buffalo situation calls for a small explanation of dates.
The miners who took such a southern route as Lasselle's could
start much earlier than those who intended to follow the northern route, because of the grass. The trip was impossible without
adequate pasture and this grew along the upper Missouri about
a month later than it did down toward the Ozarks. The way
toward Arkansas was ready by March 1; toward the Platte on
the northern route, April 1–10, depending on the weather.

March 11, there is incontrovertible evidence that Lasselle
was approaching the Ozarks. When he asked some native why
he lived in such a country the chap told him simply, because
he had been born there. Anyone who has had the great good
fortune to spend any time in the Ozarks will recognize the quiet
reductio ad syllogism of the Ozarkian, the greatest race of phi-
losophers since Socrates.

The criticism, if intended, escaped Stanislaus, who was not
staying in his place because he had been born there and found
it satisfactory.

The buffalo left Lasselle's southern route toward the end of
April, when the animals should have been just about able to
make it to the northern route to meet the northern travelers
in May and June. At one time Lasselle thinks there were about
fifty thousand extending almost as far as they could see, in every direction for twenty miles. They shot some and ate them,
but did not like them particularly. The ones I ate—rather, the
slices of one—in South Dakota about August one year, much
later than this occasion, were like tough, well-flavored, grass-
fed steer. Calves are said to be much better, but calves are
seasonal. However, it is hard to see why these pilgrims should

go unfed, unsheltered or unclothed with rifles and fifty thousand buffalo all around them. Except for a few bulls, disappointed in love perhaps, they are not at all dangerous. One can scratch the necks of the calves with impunity while the mama nods her head in approval of the fact that one knows a good calf when one sees it.

It is difficult to leave this little-known diary, because it is full of considered riches, which are, however, not particularly pertinent to the Gold Rush.

"James Dale burnt his whiskers by pouring cold water on hot grass." That simple lesson in physics must have lasted him a month or so till the whiskers were restored and he again became a man among men. There were 500 reasons, to paraphrase Edwin Arlington Robinson, why '49ers did not shave, of which 496 can be skipped—the others are that they had no time, no water, they needed the protection against the wind and (1) they didn't want to shave. Possibly this was not the entire reason why the Gold Rush drew men across a continent from Maine to South Carolina, perilously, but it may have contributed.

Eventually, between 1848 and 1851, about one hundred thousand people managed to land in the gold fields, but how many of them were actual miners is completely a matter of speculation. The contemporary accounts sound as if they were all miners, but this is an absurd exaggeration. Since returns of gold were dissipated between the customs, the express and personal carriage it is quite impossible to estimate how many persons were engaged in digging for any length of time, six months or so, during these three years. As has been mentioned, a great deal of gold never appeared in any statistics. My grandfather's watch charm is still around somewhere, uncoined, perhaps two ounces of pure gold. There must have been thousands of other such souvenirs.

In the three years—1849–51—it seems most unlikely that

there were ever as many as one hundred thousand people actually engaged in mining in California at any one time, if one discounts the people who were mining the miners—storekeepers, gamblers, a few women, outlaws, plain vagabonds and a few people who took the wise suggestion of the admirable Sherwood and started farms, in the valley where Sutter had visualized an agricultural kingdom and stubbed his toe on gold.

PART 2

The California gold field was a fairly tiny sliver of the continent in the mackerel-shaped valley, headed south, between the Sierras on the east and the coast range on the west. It should be a lake but it has some peculiarities of soil and elevation so that it manages to tip the drainage of the Sierra watershed out through the spout which the Sacramento has cut through the coast range, and in various small places, without floating off the population.

It is very rich, of course. It has been depositing fertile soil and enriched the dust of vineyards for almost as many thousands of years as the California Chamber of Commerce has been able to imagine. The same thing that makes the metal useless makes it very easy to discover. Except as pure gold and with silver and various alloys it is almost never obtainable. It makes a few unstable chemical combinations in cyanide, and in *aqua regia* (nitric and hydrochloric acid); the cyanide, in a sodium salt, is used by photographers. Its colloidal color is red so that it is used in glass to produce church windows. Except for that use, my lady's finger, and dental cavities, the domes of some public buildings, the unsuccessful treatment of alcoholics and the painting of cuckoo clocks, it is not very important to the human race. Except for coinage.

And still the stuff has upset the whole living of the world on many occasions which can be considered later. The cyanide process knocked the stuffing out of international exchange between 1890 and 1912—about one elapsed generation—lifting world output from $118,000,000 to $474,000,000 in that brief time, but not in California alone, since the other great fields in Australia, Alaska and Africa had been opened. The greatest output of California never reached $90,000,000, but it went into eight figures early—1852; $81,294,000—when that much money was considered a large sum and was actually worth at least three times what it is today, in most commodities. It may be observed at this point that as gold, this token metal, became more plentiful, the prices of useful supplies of commodities quietly accompanied the expansion in gold, silver, or money of any kind.

The simplest tools for the simplest miners were a shovel and a pan. The miner threw some sand and water into this modified dishpan and gave it a slight rotary and slowly tilting swish, allowing the top detritus to wash over the lip of the vessel. It had to be done very gently for it wanted motion at the top of the water and as little disturbance as possible at the bottom edge of the pan, where the heavy dust would settle. Gold could be counted on to be about eight times as heavy as ordinary sand, so when the lighter silicates had been floated away, the remaining mud would be considerably more auriferous, gold-bearing, than the original dirt.

After many of these washings there might be a yellow mud remaining, as big as a bean when it had been collected and squeezed moderately dry through the pores of a buckskin pouch. If the residue were as large as a good kidney bean and came to an ounce when dried, it was worth about $18. One week of this in a fairly homogeneous claim and one earned $126, unless he observed the Sabbath, which was not done too frequently.

If it happened to be a two-bean claim—and the miners seldom lingered long for less than that—it was $252. The gold was weighed in troy ounces, a troy ounce being about one tenth heavier than an "ordinary" avoirdupois ounce, so that the week's take would come to about a pound, as one weighs potatoes.

"Partners" could do this more rapidly with one of the many varieties of sluices, from the simple cradle to the Long Tom. It was in a kind of Long Tom that gold was inadvertently discovered, of course—the trough was supposed to carry off surplus water from the pond above Sutter's mill, but the cross braces detained the fatal metal. It took three men to operate a sluice of any type most efficiently—one to dig, one to haul, and a third to portion the load into the hopper and regulate the water supply. One would guess that cleaning the sluice at the end of the day was usually a joint endeavor, since the partners would be equally eager to know how the wash had come out.

Very soon, in a matter of weeks, after the enterprise had begun to justify more initial investment, there were all kinds of "patent cradles"—some of them successful and others that would have made Rube Goldberg (our contemporary cartoonist of mad inventions) and even our Patent Office, which has seen wilder ones than even a cartoonist could imagine, since it has first rights on lunatics, a bit troubled by vertigo. One device which was very successfully used somewhat later was a double-sluice. Top sluice, which may be called "A," was perforated at the balks, or crossbars, so that water and heavy sediment dripped through into a second sluice, "B." This semiprocessed residue could then be treated again with considerably more respect.

These things went into endless varieties eventually, but not immediately. One much later device had a canvas belt with reversed buckets which caught the drip at the lower end of the revolution on sluice B, the lower one, and returned the enriched ore to the operator at the top of the sluice for further treatment. But these things took many partners.

These were two that worked, for a time at least. The Patent

Office was flooded with applications on methods of separating and reducing gold and with every sort of device for discovering and mining the metal. There was often a substratum of sanity in the many proposals, of course, but most of them did not appear till much too late to benefit the '49er.

One thing they knew about from the first was mercury, or quicksilver. They should have known about the affinity of gold for mercury, because everyone had known about it for five thousand years. Gold will combine with many other metals in an amalgam, or alloy, in a reasonably homogeneous combination, which is why one can buy jewelry in any shade from white to reddish yellow, and why one can buy gold of various "karats." (An interesting word from the Arabic "qirat" meaning the weight of four grains of some Moslem seed, a system of weighing which would not be approved by Tiffany's.) With reference to gold, as is well known, it means the amount of gold, in proportion to 24, in an alloy. Pure gold, 24-k., is too soft for ornamental uses; 18-k. is usually good enough for the "solid gold" of jewelers and 10-k. for the "solid gold" of less valuable rings and watch cases, though a good many mail-order jewelers advertise "solid gold" articles and mention very unobtrusively that the "solid gold" is 10-k.—that is, it is five-twelfths gold.

From the start the miners knew enough to put mercury in the crossbars of their flumes to catch in alloy the dust which was so fine that it might have washed away merely by suspension. When the mercury was "loaded"—had become muddy or semisolid by the accumulation of gold—the excess mercury was squeezed out through buckskin or canvas and the amalgam was reduced by simple distillation—much simpler than that of moonshine whiskey, since the boiling point of mercury is about one eighth that of gold. Any clumsy apparatus would distill mercury from gold with this enormous variation of boiling points, 2600 to 357, centigrade.

It is impertinent to mention that there is a great difference between the generally physical combinations of alloys and the chemical combinations of elements in such things as the chlorides and cyanides of gold. It would also be tiresome; in the one case, one merely hits the combination over the head with a little heat; in the other one has to tempt the gold out of the cyanide or chloride by a complicated chemistry, which was, nevertheless, standardized to such efficiency that it shook world finance again a generation or so after the Rush. Anyone further interested in the cyanide reduction of gold can find three lines of formulae in the Thirteenth Edition of the Encyclopaedia Britannica, page 199, under "gold," together with a column of instructions. Fairly thick reading.

The first instruction should be that one whiff of cyanide will enable one to lift paving blocks of pure gold from the infinite streets of New Jerusalem; California still uses the cyanide method of prospecting on its mortal criminals.

Prospecting has always been lightly treated. Once you landed in California, where did you go? In the first place, one went to a gold region—usually Sacramento or Stockton, the northern and southern capitals of the Rush. The next induction, reducing of the circle, was simply to find where gold had been found lately. Then one went to the place and pitched a tent and "prospected."

These prospectors were not Doctors of Science in Geology. At the time they would not have been better off, as learned geologists went in 1849. They simply pitched as near as possible to some claim where gold had been found. There they panned for a day or two till they found something or did not and stayed or moved on according to the result.

The handbooks, which were all of the best sellers of the day, give intricate instructions about finding gold—a fair proportion belong in medieval texts about dipping rods and phases of the moon. Anyone mildly learned went to the bars of the creeks where it could be expected that the fugitive streams would have dropped their heaviest burden. But there had been so many streams in California and no geologist had arrived to identify the strata of old creek beds, which might now be ten feet above the course of the present stream. So, around Feather River, for instance, they found nuggets and even one enormous plaque of gold on hillocks that were far above the ordinary course of the stream.

Since the Baptists had created the world in 4004 B.C. (the 004 is a puzzle), they had no smallest idea of what igneous and erosive performances might have occurred in California in the millions of years when this terrain had squeezed out of rocks, exploded in its labor, and spattered the place with soft but noncorrosive gold. Dust, perhaps, but imperdurable. The creation and incidence of gold is a foolish speculation about the composition of the earth as a physical body. A vastly more important material, iron, occurs almost in a lump in the Mesabi Range of Minnesota; silver was gobbed a little east of gold in Nevada; diamonds happened in South Africa; tin occurs in Great Britain and the Malays. It is an odd pattern, my masters. A plop of this here and that there, a splatter-brush with no evident design.

The careful prospector knew a good deal more about pure empiric geology than most geologists. A good prospector had to be a geologist, geographer, and above all, an economist. One does not search for Ophir with a load of parlor curtains. They had the hardships that have been mentioned in many accounts, but most of them had gained, by hoot and by hell, a knowledge of the deadly country and its deserts and cliffs, over about the Sierras, and a sense for any gulley or broken crop that might show a sign.

One must say for these amateurs that it was amazing that they found as much gold as they did. They had no chance, the shovels of 1849 against the hydraulic mining and cyanide of

1890. There are presently various enterprises in the Mesabi Iron Range of Minnesota for the "beneficiation" of taconite, which means the ore drifted about the rich deposits and mixed in its clay—there is an opinion that this residue of the great deposit, enormously greater than the high-grade center, though not as rich, will supply the country for a thousand years. So it goes with gold.

Prospecting was a wandering business, and not principally for the romantic reason given in most accounts, that the '49ers were an adventurous lot never to be satisfied except by a true Golconda or Eldorado. If such regions had proved numerous, gold would now be used instead of the more versatile and useful tin for plating cans of baked beans and that formidable Young Bride's Helper, the exotic canosoup. There were plenty of the firstcomers—and second and twentieth-comers, as far as that was concerned—who would abandon quite good claims on the rumors of some rich creek in Oregon or the news of tremendous nuggets up on Feather River. There were such nuggets in the latter case but the trouble was that by the time the newcomers arrived, the nuggets had merely been there. For this superficial gold was quickly exhausted.

The itinerant character of the miners was chiefly due to a different faithlessness; that of their claims. There is a phrase undoubtedly from this period which still hangs around in the hospitable American language, "How did it pan out?" And the reply which means two entirely different things, according to its expression, "Oh, it panned out," dismally, or, "Oh, it panned out," enthusiastically, meaning that the project gave no returns, or gave splendid returns.

In the mines it required an auxiliary verb—when a claim panned out, it produced; when it *was* panned out it was exhausted. And most of the claims that panned out *were* panned out in an amazingly brief time. A man who could dig and pan a few hundred pounds of sand and clay a day expected an

ounce or two for his labor; he would have been incredulous
to hear of modern companies which operate comfortably by
obtaining one ounce from two tons of disagreeable blue stuff
that looks like it had solidified from fermented sewers.

The first miners were working on the superficies of the ero-
sion of the rivers. The companies who sent divers to California
to find gold on the bottoms of the streams would have found
very little, even if diving in California creeks had been very
practicable. Most of the gold in these early locations was virtually in sight, as it pretended to be. It had rolled and diffused
in most unlikely places as the rivers changed their courses;
sometimes the particles were heavy enough to drop in some
unlikely place and stay there, but for the most part the fields
of the first miners were the scattered sands of the streams, and
those were so superficial that they were exhausted in a few
months, weeks, or even days. Then the Chinese took over and
made enough out of the "exhausted" claims to become first-class
mandarins in China, or to start a chop-suey parlor in San Francisco. (The old rumor that chop suey was invented in America
about this time is almost certainly a myth; the Chinese had
been serving rice dishes, variously fortified and garnished for
thousands of years.) (On second thought, what *is* chop suey,
and why does anyone try to be iconoclastic about its Chinese
origin? You can bet the '49ers didn't think of rice and barley
sprouts.)

The dimensions of the claims show the cynicism of the miners
about the probable product. In reasonably rich strikes claims
might be limited to as little as ten feet in frontage, usually
against a stream whose banks and bed were supposed to contain any dust that might be in the vicinity. The rear boundary
was usually somewhat vague, as it was in the case of Mr.
George Washington, whose "Western Properties" apparently extended to the Mississippi River, adjoining the French Territory
of Louisiana, all the way from the Potomac.

Bancroft, in *Popular Tribunals*, gives some notion of the confused rules which obtained. The staking itself was simple enough, four pegs put in the ground and usually decorated with rags or, in the case of the wealthy, with tin cans. This was sufficient in the beginning, for the law was constituted by the society of the settlement and the penalty for infringement did not depend on the prowess of the person or persons injured. Society determined it. Claim jumping was a public matter, a threat to the community, ànd it was quite as serious as horse stealing and possibly more serious than murder, upon which most whiskey-barrel judges were likely to cast a benign eye if the slightest justification could be shown.

By a simple rule of thumb if a man did not work his claim one day in the month he was gone or dead and anyone could take over. As will be seen, when law finally reached the camps, in a very occasional manner, mineral rights superseded every ordinary property right. Anyone pursuing any clue to a gold vein could do his digging where he pleased—in anyone's cellar, if there had been any cellars, under the capitol, if there had been any capitol, beneath a church pulpit, in a graveyard. Exactly this last thing did occur when someone with a slightly macabre sense of humor salted the dirt beside a newly dug grave and went on to stake a claim on the grave. Instead of being lynched, the joker started a small rush on the graveyard —gold was where one found it.

There are so many stories of this nature in the enormous accretions of reports—letters, pamphlets, books, and particularly the early California newspapers to be found in many large libraries—that one is left to preference rather than discretion about which to accept. Since the things are of no particular historical importance except as small and frequently misleading clues to the manners of the place and time, it does not matter much whether one believes the legends or not, if he takes the precaution of disbelieving about half of them. Which half is not important, either, within the modest limits of ordinary credulity.

The whole picture, however, *is* important, but that can generally be deduced from the effects on relative events of responsible record. The Rush caused profound effects, quite disproportionate to the small discovery of an insignificant amount of the world's basic currency in a remote and unexpected location. Something was certain to happen in the tropic of California sooner or later; gold made it happen sooner.

The mild sneer at the geology of the miners is not actually deserved. The simple principles of prospecting were quickly learned, but apparently no one learned much about it beyond the mere chance presence of locations and traces; science would have been fairly helpless in a place that had been torn to pieces by everything from mountain torrents to volcanic eruptions for millions of years.

The old legend of the "Mother Lode" clung on for a long time, but apparently the mother was less maternal than explosive. There was no predicting the location of her derned infants. At long last, of course, long after the Rush, the exploiters used brute force as they do today to wash down and work the scattered particles, but no one has ever found the solid gold mountain from which these golden sands and rocks were dispersed. It is, of course, a million to nothing that the dispersion took care of any substantial source remaining.

The good locations were so scattered and so accidental, in a way of speaking, that it was beyond geology. Bancroft tells a story that is sufficiently apropos to seem credible.

Negroes had little trouble in the mines. They were few and so they were amusing; they were also pleasant with the quiet humility that is characteristic of gentlemen of any race. One of these colored fellows started picking at a bank that seemed to have been, and probably had been, long abandoned.

"Nigger! What are you doing on my claim!"

The colored man said that he was very sorry but he hadn't seen any evidence of working, and, since he was a complete stranger to the whole job, he had just taken a chance on a place where some more educated person seemed to have thought there might be gold. And he asked where the white man could recommend a location, possibly with gold but away from any possible trouble.

"Oh, up atop the ridge there," the white miner said, suggesting the unlikeliest place for both gold and trouble.

So, in some ancient shifting of the river beds, a kindly current had left a thirty-pound piece of gold barely under the grass roots where the Negro first struck his pick. This story *could* be true and I prefer to think that it is; I have seen that beautiful plaque of gold in the Rapid City (S.D.) Museum in a region where mining is done by a ton-to-an-ounce method, or worse, and that one just happened; so it did up at Feather River where a few parties yanked out nuggets, by no science or system, while a hundred others spent their days shoveling utterly barren earth.

The gold happened. Many years later they learned how to trace this stuff—to its exhaustion—in quartz formations and clays and such things, but at the time of the '49ers the creeks were God's first miners. They carried it and washed it and dropped it in the sand.

Simple problem—tramp around till one found which sand.

The treatment of the product was even more complex. Back in the old Olaf sagas there is the story, in the *Heimskringla*, of his sending a gold ornament to some Scandinavian queen he thought it convenient to marry. But her jewelers took the piece in their hands and smiled at each other. Too light. And sure enough, it was plate.

Such sensitivity seems almost incredible, but probably neither of those jewelers could have qualified as a bartender in Sonora.

The ideas of miners picking up nuggets at random or starving to death, unless by accident, are equally inaccurate. A reasonably competent and unreasonably industrious miner—so few of them were—could usually net a few thousand dollars a year. His first research was for a paying claim—as long as it paid he remained there. Grandfather Duffield spent nearly three years in the Fields; his diaries and letters mention accumulations of $3000, $1500, and $2000 over different months or quarters of this period. He changed claims several times, but always within a particular cornfield, below Sonora. He wound up with twenty or thirty thousand dollars' worth of cornfields—in Iowa; a considerable estate at that time.

But the definition of a competent miner did not apply to nine tenths of the immigrants. They kept on rushing from one "'lumne" river to another, up to Oregon, over toward the Sierras. They were nearly all very young men and the first rumor of a strike would take them from a fairly profitable claim up or down or around to "diamonds as big as the Ritz," to borrow from Fitzgerald's good story. An ounce or two a day, in a dependable location, could not contain them when they heard that nuggets as big as ostrich eggs had been found on Feather River or up in Oregon.

By the same token, most camps were as impermanent as caddis flies. At certain central points between the creeks and gulleys towns grew up. Sacramento, being the river port from San Francisco, established itself quickly and Sam Brannan, Sutter's Mormon storekeeper, managed a hotel there which earned him (says Bancroft) $160,000 a year. There are thirty or forty mining towns and more camps mentioned in early books on California—but it was a promising town where anyone would make an investment in clapboard, and these were few and far between. There were far more settlements that had names at one time or another—soon deceased.

The ordinary camp was simply a scattered assembly of tents.

If some creek or gulley showed enough promise to keep a dozen miners or so around for a year or six months, some wild speculator might invest in enough lumber to put up a general store, specializing in hard drinks in many instances.

The hard-drinking business, the gambling and general profligacy has undoubtedly been wildly exaggerated, just as American crime is exaggerated by radio and motion pictures today. Anyone following a television set or a program of attendance at movie theaters, would assume that at least three fifths of the American population consists of thieves, murderers, drunkards, call girls, muggers, rakes, and adulterers. They make more exciting stories and partly for the reason that they are *rarae aves*. So the old chroniclers of the Gold Rush, especially visiting foreigners—usually Englishmen—pictured them, and so they are still represented.

As a matter of fact, it was not till the metropolitan influx of 1849, the Sydney Ducks from Australia, the dregs of the Irish from the eastern cities, the lazy and footloose Mexicans, of their kind, all the rest of the most lawless of classes who could possibly obtain or work a passage, that crime became a problem. Hittell remarks that in 1848 there was little or no quarreling or disorder in the mines and that "theft and other crimes were almost absolutely unknown."

That changed, but not drastically. An unfriendly doctor, (*Diary of a Physician in California*, James L. Tyson, 1850) says that 15 per cent of the miners in the country were derelict from drinking and gambling and indolence, in one combination or another, or all three. Tyson based his estimate on newspaper accounts, aside from his observations, and Hittell says "this estimate is undoubtedly large."

Considering the conditions of the dismal winter for the miners, when they sat in a tent and listened to the rain for six months or so, it is not wonderful that they went to the nearest convivial assembly whenever it was possible. They were very young and active men, engaged on an adventure which was regularly interrupted for half the year, and there were no public libraries or church socials. There were no girls to go courting; there was no general store with a stove sitting in a spit pan—if there happened to be a saloon, one went there.

Maybe he became drunk and made a fuss for the greater profit of the eastern correspondents (no one has ever written about how *they* behaved) or maybe he had two beers, at one dollar each, and talked about the weather and the state of the nation. And waded back home through the mud to his tent.

Some of these accounts of profligacy are absurd per se. Johnson's *California and Oregon* tells of a miner named, economically, "Bill," who dropped a lump of gold worth "some three dollars," on a saloon floor in the course of a spree and had it returned to him by a bystander.

Bill refused it with the gracious words, "You had better keep that lump for a sample."

A "lump" of gold worth three dollars would have weighed about one sixth of an ounce and, the weight of gold being what it is, would have made no noticeable thump on the floor. Since a ton of gold is a cube slightly over 14 inches on a side, this three-dollar fragment would have been much smaller than a small pea and anyone who recovered it must have been keen-eyed.

However, the whole history of the Rush is jammed with accounts of the reckless drinking, gambling, and spending of the miners, so that the casual reader gets the impression that the whole adventure was carried out by a crowd of dissolute rakehells. As a matter of fact only about one miner in seven or eight contributed regularly to the gold sent east by the saloons and professional gamblers. Of the others, there must have been many who drank with some moderation, or took an occasional conservative fling at monte or poker or faro without endangering their plan of getting back to their real homes with enough dust to make the expedition successful; there must have been a substantial number, like my grandfather, who were total abstainers and regarded playing cards as the devil's Bible—temperance was then an issue almost as partisan and publicized as slavery.

The sober miners entertained themselves through the rainy season and the succeeding days of high water by exchanging visits between tents for gab fests, playing such innocent games as checkers, backgammon, lotto, etc., writing letters—they were great for writing letters as the terrific collections in many libraries show—doing a little desultory mining when the weather permitted, mending and repairing clothing and camps. During his two winters there Grandpa spent a great deal of time at his favorite sport, hunting, so that he and his partner and probably the neighbors must have come out of the dreary season fatter than they entered it, since later, even in his eighties the old gentleman hunted squirrels with a rifle very successfully.

The settlers from the Midwest must have found the experience merely a prolonged camping out in bad weather. They had already been through canvas covers and log cabins. In Iowa, for instance, the active season for major outdoor work—plowing, harvesting, preparing—began and ended at about the same time as that of the Fields, between April and November.

This whole picture changed, of course, in 1849, when the scum of the earth descended on the Fields from Sydney, Ireland, eastern America and Mexico. One could no longer leave his accumulation of gold in his tent unguarded all day while he went about his work. The Sydney Ducks, for instance, penetrated the Fields sometime in 1849, but being of metropolitan character they chiefly resorted to the wooden towns, from which they made forays on the camps.

This changed the character of the country; it also changed the character of the respectable miners, a decent bunch of young farmers and artisans, who now took abruptly to the pistol and the rope, with no small success, since they were very capable people. The crimes and murders and lynchings, again, have been extensively advertised, the extempore courts—where there were no authorized courts—the unusual procedures and sentences by unqualified judges.

My grandfather saw one hanging in two years and some months in his camp below Sonora. The outlaws did not bother with small camps too much, because strangers of doubtful appearance could not pass unremarked and were under surveillance day and night till they had established some integrity.

Outside the camps, in the small towns, it was different. There was constant traffic and trading in these places and one rule of the places, especially for storekeepers and bartenders, was never to ask questions.

SEVEN

"The common law is reason dealing by the light of experience with human affairs. One of its merits is that it has the capacity to reach the ends of justice by the shortest paths." U.S. 100. 584. Bouvier, Law Dictionary.

This is not a complete definition of the subject, of course—indeed, this Baldwin edition of Bouvier devotes two or three more columns of exceedingly fine type to the subject—but it was a sufficient definition for the miners, who never heard of common law but figured it out for themselves, though in some instances they made it a bit too common.

Till about the middle of 1850, when there was some effort at the organization of judicial districts in the mine country, the administration of justice in the camps was purely extempore. The miners elected a magistrate, who was called an "alcalde" as often as not, and in most cases the judges selected a jury—twelve men when convenient but sometimes as few as three. Counsel was a very rare thing; they used the French system of examining magistrates. It was also more or less the *Alice In Wonderland* system, "I'm the judge and I'm the jury—." In the main, the system seems to have worked out reasonably well in the early years. Decent and sober men presided over courts which were very anxious to preserve the evidences of their decency and due process of law, as far as it was practicable.

They grew more grim with the influx of an undesirable population. Flogging was established as a punishment for crimes meriting a rope on the back rather than around the neck, but flogging was naturally followed by exile from the camp and, since the evidences of thirty-nine to one hundred vigorous stripes could hardly be concealed, general exile. The exile could be as nearly as possible tantamount to a death sentence, for a man with his stripes, no equipment, and every man's hand against him must have had no easy struggle for survival.

In winter in the northern fields about Sacramento—the southern fields centered around Stockton—exile may have meant fairly prompt death from starvation or freezing, as is suggested in Francis Bret Harte's "Outcasts of Poker Flat." (Incidentally, both Bret Harte and Mark Twain have their names carelessly associated with the literature of early gold mining. Bret Harte was thirteen years old when the '49ers went to California and Mark Twain was in the silver mines of Nevada briefly at the time of the Battle of Gettysburg before he went to California. I have read all of Mark Twain, including "1601" and "Report from Paradise," and I do not remember that he ever wrote anything about the Gold Rush. I am not as well acquainted with Bret Harte, but he usually wrote about the 1870's.)

Murder was quite regularly punished by hanging except in the "big" cities where the Hounds and the Sydney Ducks had the law either terrified or suborned all through 1850 and during the first six months of 1851, a subject for more special discussion later. There were two exceptions to this law of the rope—it was faintly reprehensible to shoot an innocent Mexican and the citizens frowned upon such murders; I have found only one or two instances in which anyone was ever even admonished for killing an Indian or a Chinese.

In the case of the Indians this was shortsighted. They were treacherous and they were thieves; they could have become dangerous as they afterward did under Modoc Jack. But they would dig all day for a quart of very bad liquor or a handful of beads, or all week for a blanket or a scarf. Naturally they would not work any more after they had what they wanted, but there were always plenty of Indians who had seen something at the trader's and would dig a hundred times its value to get it, dig for some white man who cheated them, to pay to some trader who cheated them.

It made no difference to them; they had nothing much to do with their time and they were being introduced to strange splendor—the white man's fabrics, the white man's colors, the white man's guns and, particularly, the white man's liquor. The latter two items later led to the gruesome Modoc War.

However, it was quite all right to shoot an Indian, and if any explanation were required, to mention quite casually that the fellow had been drunk and threatening or had been stealing. The white population was a little bit uneasy about the Indians, who had the real title to the Fields, and supercilious to the Mexicans, who had the next best claim.

The only account of even mild justice for the Indians is one of a white man who killed an Indian in order to rape his squaw, which he did. The Indians caught him before he could return to civilization and dealt with him in the Indian manner, not too briefly, but finally, finally. The miners conceded that the Indians were justified—the chap sounds like someone who would not have been very popular in camp, anyway.

To the end of the Rush, and probably much longer, the Indians never learned what the reason was for the inordinate value the white men put on this yellow mud. Now flint—that was valuable!

The Chinese were quiet, humble, and inoffensive, and undoubtedly the principal aggravation they gave the miners was their enormous immigration, coupled with the fact that they insisted on remaining Chinese. This made the immigration more noticeable and it was quickly observed that if Chinese immigration continued at an increase of several hundred per cent a year California would soon be a suburb of Shanghai. There was some truth in this, but hoodlumism and murder were not the proper answers. Among the hoodlum element in the mines neither a "Chinaman's" life nor his property was safe from day to day.

Ridiculously enough, the propaganda on this matter settled on pigtails. Pigtails probably cost more Chinese lives than even their success in mining abandoned claims and making money out of them. There is some legend that Chinese preserve these pigtails because they expect to be drawn up to heaven by them; I see nothing more absurd about this than the beards of jazz musicians which point in the opposite direction.

Virtually all of the Chinese were of the coolie class, of course, and when they did not go to the mines they were assigned women's work, perhaps with subconscious reference to the long braided pigtails, which is probably why the notion that all Chinese are laundrymen, and vice versa, persists in some degree to this day directly in the face of facts.

At any rate, it was fairly safe to murder a Chinese or to jump his claim, and completely safe to insult or assault one. To some degree, as was mentioned, this was the fault of the Chinese themselves; they were even more clannish than the French, but the French, like the British, had nearly given up pigtails half a century before.

The Mexicans and Chilenos had a position in limbo. A good many of the Chilenos were skilled miners and this was resented by the less successful and responsible of the American miners and respected by the others. As soon as there was anything mildly representing law in the region, a vigorous effort was made to tax the foreigners out and this was led by the Irish and Germans who had not washed their feet since they had left the old country, if they ever had there. To be fair, the Mexicans who went north to the Fields were not the most desirable of the Mexican nationals. They were not the settlers of the country—those remained comparatively undisturbed down on their ranches in southern California till they were crowded out in

Yankee real-estate deals—nor were they simple peons. They were an adventurous class of younger men who hated the Anglo-Saxon intruders; they were at once dissolute and indolent; they were the first procurers of the northern settlements because they could manage a certain supply of women from the South; they were light-fingered and they fought with knives.

These were some of the reasons, chiefly based on temperament, why it was fairly safe to shoot a Mexican, and why it was very dangerous for the most innocent and decent Mexican to face an American stump jury.

Bancroft never vouches for his incidents, culled from the journals, reminiscences and letters of the miners, and he is wise not to do so, for some of them are the most palpable lies or reports of incredible reports. But he tells at considerable length (which indicates his belief in the credibility of the yarn) of the trial of two Mexicans for the theft of a team of mules. A miner appeared in a bar one day and said that his team of mules was missing and he had seen two Mexicans driving what he believed to be his animals.

Sure enough, two Mexicans appeared in the bar very shortly and the miner immediately identified them as the ones he had seen driving his team. A court was set up and the Mexicans were put on trial for their lives. If they had been "white" men the penalty would have been a flogging.

The Mexicans swore that they had never seen the mules and knew nothing about them. They had come from some neighboring camp on foot and had not paused at any camp between —certainly they had not stolen any mules. The miner was not certain of his identification, but he was reasonably sure that they were the same Mexicans. It might be noted that to the miners all Chinese looked alike and most Mexicans.

The mob took custody of the prisoners and the jury retired to consider its verdict.

It seems to have been a fairly honest jury for it came back with a verdict of Not Guilty.

This would have seemed to end the matter but the crowd about the bar suggested that the jury go out and consider its decision more carefully. The jury went out and returned, again with a verdict of Not Guilty.

It was then suggested that they go out for the third time and, in view of the fact that the Mexicans had already been hanged when the first verdict was returned, the jury had better find that the defendants were guilty. The jury complied. The case was further complicated by the fact that the manager of the tavern belatedly remembered that the plaintiff, hardly fit to drive himself, much less a team of mules, had left the critters in a shed behind the establishment, where they were found.

(It is to be observed in most of these early cases that there were different codes of punishment. If an American stole a mule he was flogged; if a Mexican stole one he was hanged, and in the case of the Mexican an accusation was almost as good as a conviction. "White" men were occasionally hanged for stealing, but there was strong sentiment against it.)

For unprovoked murder the penalty was the same for all races; for provoked murder, in resisting robbery or unjustified assault, there was nothing but congratulations. There were no degrees; there were no lawyers.

Only one woman was hanged in the early days of the mines, on record; she was, of course, a Mexican. A Scotsman in Downieville took too much at the bar one night after a Fourth of July affair, '51—the stuff they served was not fine old drambuie—and decided to visit a Mexican lady of the community. No further name than Juanita. The Scot was named Jack Cannon. Apparently the señora's husband or friend made no objection to the visit, but the señora stabbed the Scot neatly in the heart. She refused such formal trial as the time and place could afford her and asked them to hang her and get it over with, which they did. They noosed her to the timbers of a bridge; she flung her hat to a friend in the crowd and jumped off without encouragement. (Bancroft and Hittell differ on the details, except for the salvage of the hat.)

Apparently the execution was condoned by the whole crowd, which must have contained a good many decent people and people with plenty of courage to make a protest if anyone had wished to protest.

Now it was considered highly impolite to hang a woman in California at this time, when, outside a few towns like San Francisco, Sacramento, Sonora, Marysville and Stockton and a few others, decent women were almost revered and indecent ones were generally besought. So there must have been a strong community feeling against this Mexican lady. Perhaps she had tantrums and had used a knife before; perhaps she had disseminated what was then an incurable disease; perhaps she "clipped" her customers—for it can hardly be supposed that the Scotsman found his way to her cabin by accident, considering the small number of women to be found anywhere in these regions.

The significant thing is that a whole mob acceded to the hanging of a woman without any recorded protest. They knew that the incident would be a blot on them and their place, but they were willing to sacrifice some social standing either for revenge or to be rid of the woman or both. This seems the simplest speculation, but it is mere speculation. One thing it is quite safe to say, the señora could hardly have been an angel, though she may have become one after she jumped off the bridge. The subject is so fascinating because there could be at least five speculative approaches to it as fiction: the temperamental prostitute; the honest but exploited woman, tired of it all; the outraged woman; the homicidal psychopath; hopeless accident, etc., etc. Though the last is weak—stabbing a Scot to the heart is very accidental.

Such cruel and unusual punishments as flogging were generally not cruel at all—they were alternative to hanging. There
were no jails and there were no regular law officers; even when
the district judges came in under the authority of the state,
without a jail, what were you to do with a chap who had been
caught with a stolen horse or red-handed after a murder? Chain
him to a tree till a convenient court was next in session? And
in 1849 in most of these camps, there was no particular prospect
that any convenient court would ever be in session. So they
flogged them or hanged them, according to what they considered the merits of the crime.

There was also great resentment among the older miners
about the lawless invasions of 1849. England, having excreted
numbers of its criminals to Sydney and New Zealand, now
purified these lands by expediting their further departure to
California. At various times, England, Ireland, and Italy were
about equally guilty of using the United States for a lavabo;
the first miners, who were decent people, grew impatient with
these incursions and in deserving cases extended the emigration to Eternity.

The two circumstances—the absence of law and the implements of law—and this incursion of people who did not come
from Vermont or Iowa or Indiana, but from the bilges of
European humanity, made the decent miner slightly severe—
only slightly—no one was ever burned at the stake in California.
Hanging was the utmost penalty and it was done without any
Inquisition or London Tower or Venetian elaborations. Not to
speak of some modern German appetites or the many others.

The law was probably as good as it could have been. Ann
Williams was burned at the stake in Gloucester, England, by
due process of law less than a century earlier, in 1753, for
poisoning her husband, and even more horrible executions have
been carried out against Negroes in some southern states in
modern times, but not by process of law. About the closest the

miners, who were lawless in fact but not in disposition, ever came to such things was in the notable case of a sailor who was caught trying to rob a saloonkeeper—since the saloonkeeper was obviously also the neighborhood banker, there was some feeling, and the chap was sentenced to hang by a jury of twelve men and a judge named Nuttman.

Yet there was such feeling among the miners about taking a life coldly that the sentence was changed to a flogging and the amputation of the robber's ears. The latter infliction was performed by a surgeon. The criminal was then banished from the camp. A half mile away he stole a mule.

This time there seemed to be no new place on which to flog him, so the miners simply sent him on his way with a warning about what would happen if he were ever found in the neighborhood again. This seems, at first glance, a cruel and unusual punishment but in the first instance it saved the fellow from hanging and the exile amounted to no more than what many police forces do to this day, "Get out of town and keep traveling."

A few good jails and delegated officers of the law would have stopped lynch law in the Fields instantly, but no one was to blame for the fact that these resources were not instantly available. Some of the miners had preceded and a great many of them had instantly succeeded the acquisition of the Territory (the treaty with Mexico did not go into effect till July 4, 1848) and the business of organizing a territory three months or so away from the head of national government, was managed with the usual delays and fumblings—over many intervals of about half a year.

It was not remarkable that for three years or so the administration of public affairs and justice rested largely on the integrity of the general and local publics. It *is* remarkable that this distributed and arbitrary power was managed with such a degree of quiet judgment, some mercy, and a strict regard for what anyone knew about the formalities of common law. "Jury" is a word that one finds very frequently in the accounts of the trials—they "done their best." It would have been something more than human if, in the circumstances, a few innocent people had not suffered and a few villains escaped. That happens quite often in the best-regulated societies.

The sinister Robin Hood of the time, who probably did his countrymen in the mines more harm than any other hundred Mexican scoundrels put together, was the bandit Joaquin Murieta. Since entire books have been written about him it seems a little curious to say that not much is known about the chap, or, rather, too much is known about him to be true. Outlaws of that time could not commit crimes a hundred miles apart on the same afternoon, or evening. Any particularly daring or ruthless depredation was credited to him, till only omnipresence could have accounted for his recorded activities.

There are three accountings for his outlawry, which was obviously simply a taste for banditry. One was that his brother had been hanged by Yankees; another that his sister had been raped and murdered by Yankees; a third that his dearest friend had been hanged by Yankees on unjust charges.

At any rate, for about two years he raised the devil around the mines. He stole everything from gold to cattle, managed grand raids from San Diego to Sacramento, and threw both ranchers and miners into a dither. His first fame seems to have begun in June, 1851, and his head was put on exhibition in July, 1853.

He was certainly the Jesse James of California; his trademark was wanton and unnecessary killing, as it was that of the Missouri bandit. The dirty little coward who shot Mr. Howard and laid poor Jesse in his grave certainly rid the world of a homicidal maniac and so did the person who killed Murieta, if anyone ever did. Murieta's anonymity lay in numbers; almost any of his surviving victims would identify any tough young

Mexican as Murieta (he hoped) and the result was that almost any tough-looking young Mexican was likely to be shot or hanged without further explication. If Murieta hoped to avenge the Mexicans on the Yankee he chose a most disastrous way to do it.

Murieta is supposed to have been killed after a raid on July 30, 1853. His executioners cut off his head—a head, at least—and exhibited it, for a small fee, around the camps and towns of California. Some people said it was Murieta's head and some said that it was not. Some said he had escaped and gone to join his sweetheart—probably the one who was raped and murdered—in Sonora, Mexico. Some said he was two other people and this, paradoxically, is the probable answer, if the two is multiplied by a dozen or so. Every major gang crime was attributed to Murieta. At any rate there was a lull in gang crimes after this occasion; so possibly they did get Murieta—but that did not save a number of Mexicans from the noose or the bullet as possible lieutenants of the brigand.

If it was Murieta's head that was exhibited, he had a postmortem fate more inglorious than Hector's. Some thirsty person drank the alcohol in which his head was preserved and the head sp'iled. This was serious; it stopped gate receipts. Why the alcohol was not replaced is not explained—perhaps the attraction was giving out; also formaldehyde is a better preservative.

These incidents are about as representative of California mining society as *True Crime Stories* would be of contemporary American society. If one stuck to business and stayed away from saloons he simply dug gold instead of plowing corn. My grandfather shot one man who had jumped his claim while he was hunting; the fellow refused to move out and started to "draw." I will never know whether the shot was fatal or not. Grandpa let the basic facts slip out one evening—I was about nine—and my cousins and I assumed that he blew the cuss's brains out. I have considered the story in my later years and I imagine that because of Grandpa's further reticence on the subject our naïve assumption was correct.

This was apparently the only dangerous violence that occurred in his experience, during those remunerative years, 1850–52. A letter to his brother in Iowa says, "I have $3000 in dust. I wish it were there instead of here." His brother was assembling a farm for him in Iowa. This is the only sign of uneasiness his letters furnish and his uneasiness was probably occasioned by the fact that, as a good Methodist, he did not want to shoot anyone else. He was a medium-to-small man—they are bad business.

The villainy of the place was not intricate. A murder had to be succinct—there were no trains, autos, or airplanes, there were not even many cities large enough for any secure concealment in the region. Two of the usual motives for murder did not exist—sex jealousy or the hope of ultimate gain, for almost no one in the Fields had a wife or a will.

This left, of course, simple robbery or uncomplicated irritation. The evidences of these motives are generally too obvious to invite a sane person to crime. The remote and spacious circumstances gave some possibilities for flight, but not as many as a casual observer might consider. Where to fly and how? To dash off on a horse is the reply usually furnished by what are called "horse operas," but even the fine mounts of the Pony Express were required to dash only ten miles at a stage; there are various reports of horses doing over a hundred miles in one day, but the reports do not mention that the horses were then sent to an expensive sanitarium for the next month, and casual criminals did not keep stage stables.

The routes for flight were strictly limited. Sufficiently equipped, one could go to the mountains for a period; one could join the criminal world of San Francisco and perhaps ship away; one could go to Oregon or down to southern California, but the prospect was not pleasing in any direction. The itinerant nature of the population made it a perilous probability that anywhere within a thousand miles one might come upon a person who would remark, "Aren't you the party that was in Stinkwood Gulch just before old Jim Jones was shot—and his dust missing?"

Even with luck, it became evident a little later, in the time of the Vigilantes, that the identities and persons of people cursorily described as "suspicious," were very well known all through the mining regions. The gangster organizations of the thieves and arsonists about the cities made citizens somewhat reluctant to denounce known criminals for a time; not for long. When the Vigilantes showed their determination the Committee was overwhelmed by the voluntary reports. And even more overwhelmed by separating the veritable from the malicious.

As at the present time, crime was unprofitable away from towns and their convenient offer of anonymity. In the camps justice was almost punctiliously precise but it was drastic. Hang him or let him go. A trial that lasted over half an hour was obviously taking up valuable time.

Though the Chinese were treated as subhumans they were chiefly their own executioners. The *tongs* were set up almost immediately, but because they were chiefly Chinese killing Chinese, no one paid much attention. There was one stated battle between tongs, encouraged by the Whites, which kept the blacksmiths busy for weeks manufacturing breastplates, helmets, and spears. Since the account is easily available in Bancroft there is no use to detail it here. At a stated hour and moment the parties joined across a ditch, with the white miners applauding.

They went at it with hatchets, knives, maces, and spears. A few of them had pistols but the oriental idea of manslaughter is not just to make a pop and see someone fall over but to produce a good loud thunk manually, audible to honorable ancestor. That they were mere gladiators, amusing white devils, did not occur to them—they were fighting for the honor of their tongs. A German miner fired into the melee, merely for the fun of the thing. He was shot instantly, most probably by some white man who was a bit ashamed of the promotion of the fracas but intended to see fair play, nevertheless.

There was not much mortality, but the fighting was hard enough to produce a modicum of respect for the Chinese in the neighborhood.

The minorities suffered principally from the fact that the first Rushers had been reasonably good citizens on an honest adventure. They were as circumscribed intellectually and as intolerant as any other Methodist is likely to be, but even denominationalism has a tendency at times to tend toward decency.

The displays of constituted law were so ineffectual, even after the establishment of district judges, that on one occasion when a sheriff attempted to quiet a lynching mob by assuring it that the prisoner would have fair trial and adequate punishment if left in his custody, the crowd shouted, "Remember Tilton!" the reference being to a murderer who had escaped custody without the slightest difficulty, as was customary with many prisoners who left fat pouches in the custody of the court and were not expected to return to make any claim.

The common law of the place was drastic, but if one were admonished by the Bible not to suffer witches why should one suffer murderers and thieves? California was singularly free of witches—the kindly gentlefolk and clergy of New England had hanged or squashed them all with the sanction of regular courts. On the whole, the California roughnecks, outside the towns, seem to have been pretty decent—though practical—customers.

EIGHT

Some mistaken person once said, "Let me make the songs of a nation and I care not who makes the laws." His notion is overwhelmed by multiplicity—the laws change from minute to minute, but the songs change even more rapidly. The "Star Spangled Banner" was not stolen from a British composer's "Ixion In Heaven" because the British composer had already stolen it from an Italian operetta. Copyright laws were lax in those days.

The miners sang everything from the coarsely ribald to the nauseatingly sentimental, but there was usually an undertone of mockery. They were going through a tough siege but they did not expect it to last forever; if it did last forever it was one more job for the coffinmaker. If it did not it was Oh, Susannah on a solid-gold knee.

In general these lads were either in a slough of despondency or nostalgia, or in very high and hopeful spirits. So their songs vary from "Oh, Susannah" to laments about sunsets and broken hearts.

Their drawings, of which there are thousands extant were about on the level of those of "Boz" (Charles Dickens) and Thackeray, mere blackboard scrawls. No Goya or Toulouse-Lautrec seems to have appeared among them—a serious deprivation to them and eternity. There are, to reiterate, thousands of pictures of the mines and the miners, but all of them so caricatured or clumsy that they fall far short of a reasonable representation. And Mr. Brady and his cameras were still fifteen years away. Daguerre's method was only about ten years old and still a matter for scientists.

It was a modest recess from the manners of mankind—they would have time for those things later when the gold was dug. Preachers had a good deal of support and exercised their begging privileges to the point where one leading Baptist friar used a whole sermon to denounce a boniface who had actually charged him $5.50 for his room and board. Since ravens had quit feeding the parsons they were a bit nasty about their keep.

A number of the anointed turned into tavern keepers and did very well. Some of them mined some gold, but for several years after the height of the Rush there seems to have been a very indifferent kind of clergy in California, apart from the established Mexican priests who were less than the dust—in both senses—to the western Methodists, southern Baptists and Yankee "psalm snorters" of all varieties.

It was a year or two before religion and entertainment of other varieties made any serious impression on the camps. The first great miners in the country were certainly Caroline and William Chapman, who played all through the mines during 1852 and 1853. They were brother and sister. They seem to have been acquainted with all the routines of vaudeville; they sang, danced, and clowned and they were dearly beloved wherever they went. When Lola Montez visited the camps she did well in San Francisco but she drew poorly in the camps because the miners preferred to watch Carrie and Willie burlesque her style.

The Chapmans were occasionally endangered because the enthusiastic audiences hurled gold pieces and pouches of gold dust at them, but they were agile and did not seem to mind. A few ounces of gold dust in a leather pouch would make a very splendid silencer, but the gifts were not intended homicidally and the Chapmans must have left California with their pockets bulging. There seems to be no further record of their theatrical

careers after they left California—they must have been millionaires or better and millionaires have always been hard to trace,
even before the invention of income tax.

Lola Montez is easier to trace; several books have been written about her. She was an Irish girl named Eliza Gilbert and
she peddled what she had to barter half around the world; her
principal success was that of becoming the mistress of Ludwig
of Bavaria, who was kicked off his throne because of her; she
tried to reign for him and did not make a success of it. (Her
whole name was Maria Dolores Eliza Rozzana Gilbert—Mrs.
James, Heald, etc.) She was once prosecuted for bigamy in an
English court but this did not discourage her from marrying
Patrick Purdy Hull of San Francisco, a newspaper operator. She
was 35 at the time she reached the Fields.

She was impetuous—she once threw the unhappy Purdy
down the stairs and through the hall door and then threw his
suitcases and possessions on top of him from the bedroom win-
dow. What Purdy had done or what became of him is not recorded in history, but it is probably a timely warning not to
marry former wives of British Army officers and ex-mistresses
of Bavarian kings. The discipline is too stern for the ordinary
American being kicked down his own stairs.

After an unhappy debut in London Lola, who had performed
successfully in most of Europe, particularly Bavaria, went west.
Her general failure there was possibly because of the assiduous
attentions of the Chapmans, who naturally declared war on her
at first instance, but it was more probably because she was a
poor dancer, singer and actress, and when the miners put out
dust they wanted something for it and they didn't give a damn
about the whole state of Bavaria if the wench couldn't dance.

After her marriage to the newspaperman Lola settled in
Grass Valley, California, and set up a salon—one "o" please—
which was accepted in the neighborhood. There are dozens of
stories about her which have been recited before now. She liked

to dance on the dewy morning grass without panties or anything else; she could outcuss a teamster—she seems to have been
a true Celt. After five years in Grass Valley she moved on to
Australia, which was then having a new Gold Rush—and how
Lola could smell gold! She died in 1861, when she would have
been about forty-three.

Yet she had the discrimination to set one of our great American actresses on her way. Somewhere in the camps she ran into
a little under-teen-ager and took her under the Montez wing.
After Montez had moved, the little girl came under the tuition
of an Italian with the un-Italianate name of Mart Taylor. This
waif of the mining camps, Lotta Crabtree, died in 1924, in
Boston, leaving four million dollars. Gold is where one finds it
and Lotta did not have to dig deeper than her honest talents.

It is interesting to notice that these rough Gold Rush customers also never needed to dig much below the brain lining to
come upon sound aesthetic sense and critical judgment. Perhaps taste just happens and learning is vain. I have seen
Paderewski play to very indifferent applause in Des Moines,
Iowa; de Pachmann to noisy applause, and Harold Bauer to
the greatest applause—momentary silence.

A young bookkeeper from Pennsylvania named Stephen
Foster was forming the musical tastes of the nation at this time
with lush southern ballads—about as close as he ever came to
the South was Cincinnati. He wrote most of his own verses as
well as the accompanying music and, though the verses were
generally quite bad, there was enough facile harmony to his
music to impress a whole generation of balladists, so that the
melodic style of the Rush, when it departed from hymn tunes,
which generally have no melody at all, was quite frequently
traceable to Foster.

If not to Foster, then to English or Scotch folk tunes as old
as "Barbara Allen," of whom it has been said that it was a good
thing her lover died because even as a song she has had at

least a hundred children. Sometimes they wrote new verses
to music from popular songs imported from the East. Thus
"New York Gals" reappeared as "Hangtown Gals":

> They're dreadful shy of '49ers
> Turn their noses up at the miners,
> Shocked to hear them say "Gol darn it,"
> Try to blush but cannot come it!

Chorus: Hangtown Gals are lovely creatures,
> Think they'll marry Mormon preachers,
> Heads thrown back to show their features,
> Ha! Ha! Ha! Hangtown Gals!

> To church they very seldom venture—
> Hoops so large they cannot enter!
> Go it, Gals. You're young and tender,
> Shun the pick-and-shovel gender!

For one of the most romantic periods in the age of romantic literature and sloppily romantic music, the miners were
strangely skeptical about the girls they left behind them. "The
Lousy Miner," of which one stanza has been quoted, beyond
describing a prevailing sanitary condition with considerable ac-
curacy, is only one song of many suggesting that all the sweethearts left in the East or South had probably married deacons
shortly after the Argonaut's departure.

"Clementine" was so popular that Bayard Taylor mentions
that crossing Panama he found the native boatmen singing the
hit, with only the vaguest notions of what the English words
meant. They probably thought it was the Yankee national an-
them. And the overlanders were probably somewhat consoled
by hearing a song about the Panama or Cape Horn route which
quickly got back from San Francisco, at least as far as Fort
Laramie:

> The Captain goes to dinner
> And begins to curse the waiter;
> Knocks him out of hearing
> With a thundering big potater.
> The cabin-maid, half-crazy, breaks
> The meat dish all to smash
> And the steward comes a-running
> With a plate of moldy hash.

Chorus: Then come along, come along,
> You that want to go;
> "The best accommodations"
> And "the passage very low."
> Our boats they "are large enough,"
> Don't be afraid,
> The *Golden Gate* is going down
> To beat the *Yankee Blade.*

The early prose literature of the Fields was strong enough to make a burro cry. It was strictly journalistic, either in actual diaries, letters, or newspapers. There was not too much time for writing and little for publishing, so the characteristic style developed was succinct, often violent or ribald, and rich with the robust figures of exaggeration or understatement that dwelt with the western writer—and even crept back East as far as New York City—long years after the '49ers. It would seem more economical to call a man a scoundrel rather than "the rabid, illegitimate son of a six-toed polecat," but it was not proportionate in effect.

Some of this may also have drifted westward naturally from the East, as far as newspapers were concerned, for it was not long after this that Philip Vane, then mayor of New York, while shaving, noticed with calm amusement that William Cullen Bryant was caning an opposition editor on the sidewalk below his bedroom.

However it may have been, there is no doubt that this literary vigor in the hands of great men contributed to the writing of such men as Mark Twain, Bret Harte, Bill Nye, Ambrose Bierce, and even Eugene Field. They turned "mule-skinning" into an art which removed hide with scalpels rather than broad-axes.

One of the earliest humorous devices was pretended illiteracy. Possibly James Russell Lowell's *Biglow Papers* were not entirely responsible for this but they certainly sanctified the method—misspelling, homespun grammar, an air of simple but ineluctable common sense. Artemus Ward used the trick somewhat later; Will Rogers, the general principle, still later. Gold Rush journalist "Squibob" (Lieutenant George H. Derby) not only used the method but boasted that he had the biggest nose in California, long before Jimmy Durante was born. Hollywood seems to have been a bit late in some of its gimmicks.

The best one can say for Gold Rush writing is that it seems to have furnished an approach, or revived one for American writers, which had been somewhat neglected by eastern elegants, and returned Swift, Byron, and the somewhat overelegant Pope, in American revisions, to the attitudes of our literature and to the adventures it had acquired and endured.

NINE

Though covered wagons still trooped across the Plains for years after the migration of 1848–50, an Overland Mail was established for regular coach and mail service in 1850. This went from Independence and Kansas City to Santa Fe and Albuquerque and from there to Stockton, avoiding most of the Mojave desert, and ducking neatly between the worst of the Coast and Sierra Nevada Ranges and missing Los Angeles by less than a hundred miles. It seems incredible, but most of our present motion-picture stars had not yet been born, or the tourists might have taken a chance on the pass below Victorville to gape at the wigwams.

This was a considerably longer route than the one the wagoners, the well-advised ones—followed north of Great Salt Lake, but it had the advantage of being reasonably passable in all seasons. Nevertheless, in May, 1851, one of the many Overland Mails took the shorter and more favored route from Kansas City to Salt Lake City; then by a sharp loop, around the north of the Lake and so to Sacramento.

Carrying the mails was, of course, an operating financial necessity for these companies, but the coaches could carry—or partially fly—eight passengers, and, as early advertisements said, forty pounds of luggage exclusive of firearms and blankets. But even with government support the first Overland Mail to California lasted in its entirety only about five years, till 1854, when the branch out of Salt Lake City turned south to the finally recognized city of Los Angeles, which then sent the pilgrims on up to San Francisco.

One says "partially fly" because the coaches still rode on leather springs, though the ride was mildly improved by the invention of the "thoroughbrace." This was simply a steel bar which ran the length of the vehicle between axles, so that if one wheel hit a rock or a pit the corresponding wheel was constrained to accompany it, diminishing the sway and the swerve. This gentle device was not created for the passengers but for the comfort of the mules or horses, who thus had a more nearly even pull on the tugs. However, if the passengers reached Stockton incompletely mashed that was an extra benefit.

The turn south from Salt Lake City was made in May, 1854, at the same time the northern route was discontinued, and was, of course, made because the northern track varied from dangerous to impassable in the winters. This time the stages went southwest or south of southwest to the neglected Los Angeles, where the gentler of the folk could get boats to San Francisco —no mail-coach route was attempted from Los Angeles to San Francisco for four years, till 1858; but there must have been a great deal of courier travel between the two places, since the horseback routes had been established for more than two centuries.

The northern route from Salt Lake City to the mines endured till 1860—from 1854-60 it fed the Los Angeles trail and also after 1858 a much shorter alternative route *south* of the Lake directly to Sacramento. The routing was as complex as that of railroads. The first route, through Albuquerque, was more or less all-weather. The second, north of the Lake, made much better time in good seasons. The third route, south of the Lake to Sacramento, saved more time than either—but this was nearly on the Donner trail and was also subject to weather. It lasted only three or four years till William George Fargo and

his partner, Wells (Henry), took over the whole business of
western express, by degrees, beginning in 1851.

The first enterprise of these partners was a sufficiently well-
organized express from New York City to Buffalo. But after
1844 they had seen the handwriting on the wall as far as eastern traffic was concerned, and they had inched westward out
of the reach of the railroads. They had the principal direct
service from New York City to Buffalo at that time, but there
was a direct rail route from New York—or even Washington—
to Boston and from Boston to Buffalo. From the Atlantic to the
Great Lakes it was fairly evident that the gaps between the
eastern network and a fair web of roads already connecting
Cincinnati, Cleveland, Detroit and Chicago in the eastern Midwest would be filled immediately and the coaches would be
mere Toonerville trolleys between places which were not
joined, or inconveniently joined to the larger centers. As a matter of fact they did a thriving business in this line on short hauls
for twenty or thirty years afterward, till the railroad web was
complete east of the Mississippi.

But small stuff was not the notion of Mr. Fargo or Mr. Wells
and the country west of the Mississippi was obviously a long
way from having railways, in spite of its rapidly increasing importance. Still, it was also a long way from having sufficient
mail coaches and in 1851 Mr. Wells and Mr. Fargo set in to
repair this difficulty.

Against the feeblest competition they took over the Far West
in magical time. They began by tying up the Panama route. By
1852 their receipts were as good as U.S. currency throughout
the mines, and undoubtedly more easily available for large
sums. This naturally made them bankers as well as freighters.
They gave their notes for receipts, representing gold they had
accepted for transfer, and these notes could be cashed anywhere from San Francisco to New York City.

What was eventually known as Wells-Fargo grew to be the

largest shipping organization in the West within ten years.
Many of the overland companies collapsed immediately when
the railroad went through in 1869 and so did the Wells Company, as far as coach travel from New York to San Francisco
was concerned; but the railroad was only a single gut from
Kansas City to San Francisco, and in the developing country
many intermediate points were growing from Oregon to Texas.
So the Wells Company was not seriously afflicted by the iron
horse. Its history from 1869, long after the three or four years
of the Rush, has been thoroughly documented and is not pertinent here.

At any rate there were fairly secure routes for people to reach
the Fields if they could raise the fare. The complex of Overland
Mail routes is shown in the Atlas of the Historical Geography
of the United States, published by the American Geographical
Society and the Carnegie Institution, a magnificent volume.
These are only the mail routes; a complete map of regular
routes which did not carry mail would have bewildered the
smartest spider in the world by 1851.

It is no compliment to American enterprise that the first conspicuous stage robbery did not occur till 1856. The event which
was forefather of an industry that launched a hundred thousand pulp books and filled several billion pages of magazine
literature; which set the movies on a proper track—that event
did not occur till six years after there were stages to rob. Even
the redoubtable Murieta seems to have left stages unharmed.

The Indians were probably responsible for this. Because of
them the carriages were ordinarily rather heavily guarded
against possible assaults by the Sioux on northern courses and
the Apaches on the southern routes; also, nearly every male
traveler and many females traveled armed, so that a stagecoach
was a small cruiser on wheels. They also used good horses or
mules, so that over any considerable stretch they could outdis-
tance the decadent Arab quarter ponies. (A quarter horse is

one that can run like the devil for a quarter of a mile but
will drop dead at the end of a mile. The plains ponies used by
the Indians were nearly all from the fine Spanish Arabs but
consistently bred down by the Indian till they had already become the wild mice one still encounters in the West.)

After six years, however, the bandits learned the technique.
A coach robbery had to be done in numbers; it was later used
successfully in train robberies, and it is an ordinary military
tactic. The assaulting party was covered by concealed flanks.
The brave boys told the guards to halt and hand over; if they
reached for a gun they were shot from the brush. This arrangement was as old as military history but it took six years for
the robbers of stagecoaches to think it up—an awful blot upon
American invention.

The probable perpetrator of this maneuver, Tom Bell, was
hangèd the same year but he had been tactically correct.

If there is no monument to Tom Bell a grateful movie industry should put up a mausoleum to the fellow with William
S. Hart for designer. After this pioneering effort, stage robbery
quickly became ordinary, though not as common as our friends
of the cinema would have us believe. The guards were the
toughest gunmen the companies could employ—which probably kept a good many of them on the lawful side of the fence
—and the drivers have been described as half alligator and half
wildcat. Mark Twain mentions one who cried bitterly after an
Indian attack—his new suit had been shot so full of arrows that
it could not be mended.

Mark Twain recognized the breed of drivers immediately,
some ten years later when he and his brother and his brother's
Unabridged Dictionary—the villain of the journey—traveled
from St. Jo to Nevada. Sam Clemens had been a Mississippi
pilot and he recognized the lordly drivers as the plains counter-
part of those imperial creatures.

By 1858, and probably almost as early as 1850, the mail contracts called for an average of one hundred miles a day—twenty days from St. Jo to San Francisco but they ordinarily averaged about one hundred twenty-five miles a day and made the trip in about fifteen days—a day or two more or less. The charge was $150 in Mark Twain's time which, regarding money values, was about the same as a flight to Paris now.

But for those times, when the rumbling schooners left Independence in the spring hoping to reach Hangtown before the Sierra snows, the coaches were magic carpets; very rough magic carpets, but, then, no one has ever told us of how the Arabian transport rode. From such pictures as are available (not photographs) one surmises that air passengers of Haroun-al-Raschid's time, by roc or carpet, probably had use for those containers that are supplied to plane passengers, when needed, at the present time.

The exemplary strategy of Tom Bell made the way easy for train robberies a little later, of course. After firing a few thumping arrows at the iron horse without effect, the noble red men contented themselves with stealing telegraph wire for ornaments, and ties and spikes for fuel and adzes. The white *banditti* blocked the tracks and, working in gangs, took over the express cars and sometimes the passengers. Great train robberies are possibly somewhat more famous in vulgar fiction than great coach robberies. More organization and more loot; also, *The Great Train Robbery* was one of the first, if not the first, colossal production of the movie industry, abetted by Miss Mary Pickford, the first of America's sweethearts, and, one reflects nostalgically, not without reason.

The most spectacular effort in communication was the Pony Express. This does not belong in a story of the Gold Rush, because it was not initiated till April 3, 1860, five or six years after anything one could reasonably call a rush and eleven years after the '49ers. It lasted only about a year and a half, when the electric telegraph made it unprofitable but during its brief operation it carried the news of the Secession and the bombardment of Fort Sumter.

The ponies were not ponies, naturally. They were thoroughbred, or largely thoroughbred; they were racehorses and not little desert scrummagers. They covered the 1980 miles from St. Jo to Sacramento in eighty days—but this has nothing to do with the Rush, when the Yankee Trader, mentioned before, told his sister, "Don't send a letter by messenger—they go to the mines or go to the devil." The Overland Express corrected this situation in some part but even in Mark Twain's time it is mentioned that when a thoroughbrace on the coach broke, the driver calmly unloaded "a small pyramid" of mail and mentioned that he would send a guard back for it from the next station, till following coaches could pick it up. He also noted that the Sioux needed reading matter to keep them contented and peaceful. Since virtually none of the Sioux could read— none of the Indians of America ever had a written alphabet before Sequoia—it is obvious that the driver was being jocular. It is likely that the services of Wells and Fargo, in 1851, were considerably more conscientious than those of Mark Twain's outfit, ten years later. Sam was off on a branch route up to Nevada, but the main routes were regularly shipping gold, a few million dollars a year, a considerable part of $10,000,000 in '49, four times as much in '50, nearly twice as much as that in '51, $81,250,000 in 1852, long before Samuel's time. The business immediately grew too large for small sniping; Wells-Fargo had the best horses and carriages and much the toughest drivers in the West. They wrecked bandit gangs by employing their leaders for agents and they achieved reasonably safe transit all the way from the Missouri to the Sacramento.

Mark's story of J. A. Slade is exemplary—in 1861 he was by far the most feared man in the West—and he was also the principal agent of the Overland Express which Sam and Orion Clemens rode to Virginia City. Slade killed some 26 men, it was reported to Sam Clemens, which would put him well in the class of Jesse James, Billy the Kid, and almost any individual killer, outside the Armed Services, in American history. As long as Slade confined his efforts to people who disturbed the Overland Expresses his mortal deeds were generally applauded; but he shot a number of citizens for personal reasons and they finally hanged him.

This was very nearly ten years after the Rush, but it must be noticed that there had not been a conspicuous mass murderer between Murieta and Slade. A good many murders were committed in the interval and a good many men were hanged for them. Necessary murders were ignored, naturally. The really bloody times did not come till the coaches disembarked loads of eastern mobsters on the western cities. The foreign murderers were fairly under control by 1853, chiefly because of the Vigilantes, but the toughs increased enormously in the cities.

The district attorney's report of 1853 says that in the San Francisco District, 1200 people had been murdered between 1850 and 1853 and there had been one *legal* execution for murder. That there must have been hundreds of illegal executions goes without saying. Helper's *Land of Gold* gives a considerably darker picture. He believes, without reciting authority, that 4200 people were murdered between 1849–54, 1200 committed suicide, and 1700 became insane. The criminal records of 1855 show 538 people dead by violence—which was probably about half of them. This is in the metropolitan district alone.

California's median population during those years must have been around 200,000—100,000 or so in 1850; 380,000 roughly in 1860. One considers these enormous crime ratios—forty or fifty times those of New York City at the present time—somewhat dubiously. It must also be remembered that anyone who was executed by due process of unauthorized law was also considered to have been murdered. The rates of suicide and insanity have already been mentioned. It was moderately strenuous and even desperate country. Still, Helper's figures seem high.

A racial note for what it is worth if anything. Of the 538 dead by violence in 1855, in the San Francisco district, 370 were white, 133 Indian, 32 Chinese, and 3 Negro. This totals 538—a careless writing in my Britannica (Thirteenth Edition—the good one—) makes the number 583, which doesn't "jibe."

That the coming of the coaches meant the arrival of a largely undesirable population, including the hysterical journalists of the time, goes without saying. Also the wagons furnished a swift mode of exit. The substantial citizenry of California, the farmers, who had begun to trickle into the Sacramento Valley with the first miners and into the Oregon Territory long before that, had to drive their own outfits, of course. They needed their equipment, much beyond the capacity of the swifter transportation, and their own animals. But a loose lady or a gambler from St. Louis or Kansas City could make the green pastures of Sacramento or San Francisco in three weeks, a little more or less, and pull stakes at the same speed. If one used a certain amount of discretion about murdering someone in San Francisco on Thanksgiving there was little reason why he should not celebrate Christmas in St. Louis or even New Orleans. Before the coaches one would have been confined within one horse-day of travel and without resources to get beyond that circumference.

For some reason, probably because of crowding, the coach routes were not too much favored by returning miners after 1851. There are various references about catching a boat to Panama or even the Horn. The first traffic of Wells & Co. was across Panama, on their Far West services. My grandfather Duffield did not leave the Fields till 1852, when the Overland coaches were well established, but he chose to go back to Philadelphia by the Horn. Since he had some gold to mint in Philadelphia, where he would take train and boat almost to his final destination in Iowa, this extended journey was probably not too extravagant—anyway, he liked to go places and see things. The boat service was fairly decent by this time—especially for a buck who had served two years in the mines and come out with his skin and a pouch.

There were so many tails dragging on the road east from California that a gentleman who had grabbed what he wanted, and sent it to Iowa, and remained in good health must have earned the respect he demanded and obtained the remaining fifty-seven years of his life. Inoffensively, but he had seen the elephant and put it out on corn, unlike the eastbound traveler of the early Rush who said, "I have seen the elephant and et its ears."

Seeing the elephant, as has been mentioned, was going on some unusual enterprise not common to the neighbors.

Grandpa's trip was not as dilatory as it sounds. Western Iowa was hardly settled at all in 1852. His quickest route homeward would have been by coach to Kansas City, down the Missouri to St. Louis, up the Mississippi to Keokuk, and up along the Des Moines River to Keosauqua. The last part of the route, from St. Louis, would have been nothing new to him and Cape Horn was. So. He was an old gent of about forty filled with bituminous curiosities—he had gone out on the Panama route—his adventure had given him lifelong security in his home place in Iowa—he hadn't seen the East of the United States.

Half derring-do and half careful sobriety. People of this sort in the gold mines repulsed the metropolitan influx that came with the coaches. They organized their camps and they were particular about the parties who entered them. The administration was dictatorial but it was democratic. They did not like doubtful persons with no visible means of support and they threw them out. They were very sensitive about the inadequacy of legal operation in early California. No one, appar-

ently, was ever a Hitler in the mines. There had to be a jury
even if it was the whole camp. Even if it was a case of "Let's
try him a while before we hang him."

The traffic was not all one-sided. No sooner had the coaches
set up relatively easy transit from the Fields to St. Joseph and
from there, via St. Louis, to Philadelphia than a chap appeared
at the New York Assay Offices with a brick of gold that weighed
2319 ounces—that is, about $42,000—cast from the produce of
his diggings. This he wished to have appraised because he
wanted to put it on display. Because he wanted to put it on display he asked the officers to take their samples from the least
conspicuous spots, preferably the corners.

They did, and affirmed the value of this approximately 14-
pound (troy ounces) cast of the metal. The gentleman then
took it to a bank both for custody and because he wished to
borrow $6000 to start his exhibition. This was loaned eagerly
and it was suggested that on this substantial security he could
borrow considerably more.

No, no—this would be plenty to start his show. He would
pick the thing up when he had made his preparations and pay
off his debt from receipts. This moderation would have laid
any doubts to rest, if there had been any doubts. There was
the certificate of the Assay Office on the weight and value per
ounce, so the brick went into the vaults without further examination. If there had been the slightest examination by even
an amateur physicist the bankers would have learned that, by
its dimensions, this was the lightest gold that had ever been
mined.

Because of the moderation the borrower had showed on his
loan there was no suspicion for months, by which time the
swindler could, of course, have reached China by easy stages.
The brick was principally lead, naturally. The slightest boring
would have revealed its false content (as it did that of the
Cardiff Giant years later) but boring would have marred it

for exhibition and besides, the fellow had asked for only $6000 against $42,000 "security." If he had asked for $12,000 the bank might have had a jeweler in, but no one could be suspicious of a swindler who refused more than the pittance he had accepted for operating expenses.

If the bankers had only realized it and had not, perhaps, been reluctant about divulging the circumstances, they could easily have earned back their money by exhibiting the brick as a warning to anyone who thought of buying a gold brick. But it would have embarrassed the bank. They probably had the thing melted up for the few hundred dollars of gold that covered it and the few dollars worth of lead it contained.

The Great Original American Gold Brick would be invaluable now; any collector would pay its apparent value for the thing, duly authenticated. It led to the sales of thousands of gold bricks which continued well into the twentieth century—if they do not still continue. The sale of the Brooklyn Bridge has been virtually discontinued after a relatively brief success, though the Spanish Prisoner, the Drake Estate, the Recovered Delivery, and scores of swindles still operate. The business of giving security for the right to keep guardianship over $10,000 for a short time is still promoted, but the great-grandfather of them all was the simple gold brick and that never came into full fruit till the excitement of the Rush and the preoccupation with gold.

The gold schemes that were foisted on easterners were beyond counting. Any sturdy old miner, with whiskers and roughly dressed, with tanned and weather-beaten skin—the dermal properties could be achieved in a few months in California—could show a few nuggets from a buckskin pouch and state that these were only a few of those he had collected from a secret lode before his money ran out. He had saved just enough to return east and get some backing.

Since these operators were far from the Fields it was ridicu-

lous to ask for credentials; anyone could see that this was just
a sturdy, honest, old miner who needed a quartz crusher or a
long flume to open up the wealth of the earth. Some of these
honest old miners had never been nearer the mines than
Fourteenth Street, but some of them had seen the elephant,
knew the geography and the language and the techniques of
mining, and were very plausible.

The same system has been used in recent times, principally
on oil. If it has not already turned up in uranium, don't be
impatient. It soon will. The project did not need to seem too
reasonable; to invest a few dollars and then get a return of
thousands or a million—why, if even one comes in!—but one
never came in and if it had it would have produced an inferior
grade of severely used hot air.

A small sample of nuggets, gold-bearing quartz, or dust was
the most precious possession an eastern con man could own.
Nuggets were standard implements of the swindler—they were
more impressive than dust, in spite of the fact that very little
of the gold turned up in nuggets. There was that enormous
nugget that was found along the Feather River in '49 or '50
when that Rush was on. It weighed 161 pounds, minus 20
pounds of quartz, slightly over 2000 ounces troy, and was worth
probably $38,000, since such nuggets were virtually pure gold.

The reports about it were worth at least a million to the entrepreneurs back East. The find was represented as exemplary
rather than phenomenal—Hittell believes this was considerably
the biggest nugget ever found in California up to his time
(1898). Larger ones were later found in Australia, and the largest, apparently, in South Africa.

Thus came about the gentle interchange made possible by
the Overland, in which the East shuffled off a good deal of
undesirable population, and the West, though it did not profit
by it, furnished a means for digging gold in the East without
lifting a shovel. Some of the easterners did not stay at home

to be swindled. The merchants of Yreka, California, salted the streets with dust to encourage settlement. All one had to do was to go in front of the supply store or the hotel, dig up a panful of dirt from the street and find traces. This showed that the hills and streams around were filthy with the stuff—and there was a new customer, as long as he lasted. At Columbia they salted a graveyard, as has been mentioned, where there was most likely to be fresh digging.

The most delightful cheat of all was the company formed to mine the sands at the mouth of the Sacramento River. These were purplish black, which almost surely indicated the presence of gold, and the sands were illimitable. The prospectus for a company which was to provide washing facilities suggested that investors could hope for not less than $43,000,000 in profits.

Unhappily, like the Walrus and the Carpenter, they came to weep about such quantities of sand; forty maids with forty mops, or flumes, could not have washed out enough sand to pay their wages—the greatest miner in the world, the ocean, had taken care of that business. The black was all right, there was gold, but an ounce of gold will furnish all the reds for a cathedral's windows, or all the black stain for a whole beach of sand. Colloidal gold dispersed through glass is ruby colored—an ounce of gold may be hammered out to cover 189 square feet—a *gram* of gold can be drawn out two miles; it takes 28.35 grams to make an ounce.

Perhaps, after all, the West did not fare too badly in these transactions. Skinning an easterner was a perfectly legitimate sport and "salting" was as old as history—the salting of gold perhaps the oldest of all, as a practice, though the term is not traced by the Oxford English Dictionary beyond 1864, which is far too late; the word "salting" was well known in California fifteen years before that and it must have had an ancestry. The medieval alchemists salted their alembics to keep up the interest of their patrons in the Philosopher's Stone, though they certainly did not use the term "salt." It is a mysterious word in this usage, though it probably started about the time the mines did. It obviously derives from the use of salt as a seasoning.

The simplest method of salting was merely to sprinkle choice dust over a worthless claim; or it could be dug under a little way so that the fraud was not too ostensible, or it could be shot into a clay bank so that the customer would know it was veritable by the evidence of his own shoveling. There were a dozen ways.

The circumstances brought about by the new communication were very interesting in some aspects, but beyond this picaresque angle was the fact that a moderately dependable transport drew decent citizens to California, also, and usually delivered the mails in a few weeks, rather than months.

TEN

There is a general notion that the California of Rush days, at least in the Fields, consisted of nothing but miners and their predators, and the history of rural California as we now know it has been much neglected. Many of the early settlers who had no taste for mining or were too old for that strenuous life, accompanied or preceded the Argonauts on the reports of good grass and good land, and most of the farmers fared better than most of the miners.

They had their history, too—the Squatter Riots, the Potato Depression, the Sluice Wars. The farms were part of the mining history; one of the last violent struggles in the Rush days was that of farm vs. flume, involving small armies of embattled farmers against the companies who diverted their water and spilled useless clay and gravel over their fields and in their streams.

It has been mentioned that Sutter regarded the discovery of gold on his property as an unmitigated catastrophe. He already had great rich fields of grain and great herds of cattle; there is no doubt that he intended an agricultural export empire. This was well considered; San Francisco was obviously to be a great trading port in the oriental trade, and if it had not been for gold there would surely have been a Sutter Line of freighters, carrying grain and salt beef to Shanghai to exchange for spices, silk, and tea.

Our young Yankee merchant, who had more taste for the flute than the shovel, wound up running a dairy farm. A good many others must have followed his example and used the shovels which had been unprofitable in the creeks on the less spectacular but, for them at least, much more profitable soil of the pastures. The news of rich land in California had preceded the news of gold and there was a fair scattering of American farmers around San Francisco when the '49ers arrived. Sutter had been very willing to sell or lease farms on his enormous principality—what good is an empire without population?—and the Mexican proprietors of tremendous ranches had been quite glad to take fifteen cents an acre for 100 acres or so, here and there, of their holdings—acres which they had never seen and never expected to see.

After all, there are now 11,000,000 acres and more of usable California, so 40 here or even 160 there made little difference. The problem of government land also raised its unhandsome head; the tendency of the first farmer settlers was to consider everything in California government land and subject to free settlement, unless the proprietor happened to be actually standing on it. With a gun.

In addition there was the difficulty that deeds had to be checked against Mexican records, not only of sale but of origin and after the cession of California to the United States the records got into sloppy condition; then, the United States was dilatory about sending competent clerks who would have had some time to spend in reaching the premises at best—it was a beautiful mess which took thirty years or so to resolve, if, indeed, a good deal of California is *still* not occupied by squatters, or people with squatter deeds, or deeds founded on pre-emption. This is hardly true of southern California, where Mexicans with grants sold out at the Annexation and returned to Mexico.

With the titles so obscure, California was a broad invitation to landless people, and the reported richness of its land brought hordes of broken people pouring in; some worthless, some unfortunate, and some speculating on an enterprise less dangerous and tiresome than the digging of gold. Land speculators arrived in San Francisco almost as soon as the '49ers reached the Fields, though they confined themselves chiefly to town real estate, but farm settlers were already around before the '49ers and even at the time of the unsung '48ers—the agricultural adventurers preceded the gold seekers.

A gentleman who is identified by Buffum as an "old German named Schwartz" had a small farm on the Sacramento, a few miles below the town, in 1848. In the spring of 1849 he planted a few acres of melons; a little later he carried these to Sacramento and got one to three dollars apiece for them, according to size, and realized thirty thousand dollars on his melon project alone in one season.

It took my grandfather two years to make this much at digging and he was very fortunate—it is small wonder that he realized that there were better things to be dug than gold, and in better circumstances, so that on a short vacation to Iowa he quietly decided to stay there. The markets for farm products were not as good in Iowa but they were good enough. Most of the average-to-good miners did about the same thing—with a reasonable pouch they went back to their homes to visit, suddenly observed that their twenty or thirty thousand dollars which had seemed so miserable in a place of many millionaires, mostly mythical, made them squires at home, and never went back to California.

But some of them retired from the mines and stayed in the state as ranchers. When Captain Marryat visited the place in 1851 he found flourishing farms instead of the unrelieved wilderness and desert he had anticipated. He was impressed by the division of the great Carillo rancho, whose owners had simply left it and returned to Mexico. Part of it was covered with oats; part of it was being plowed by the Americans who had promptly seized the abandoned land. "As slothfulness and ignorance stepped out, intelligence and industry usurped their place." In short, the Americans, who considered farming an honorable and expert occupation were going to take over from the Spanish Americans, who disdained farming.

The peons of California have done fairly well at their menial labors and did from the first. One fellow near Sacramento had the idea of selling his melons by the slice; a one-pound slice for a dollar. He made twenty thousand dollars on his first crop, which is not remarkable since this retailing brought him about twelve dollars a melon. Marryat was right; these vulgar fellows who were not above a bit of plowing promptly crowded out the *caballeros,* except as the proud Castilians have returned to sell painted pots and jumping beans in downtown Los Angeles.

The agricultural development of California was retarded by the stubbornness of the weather, which refused to conform to the planting patterns of Ohio and Illinois. A place which had no noticeable rain all summer was obviously no good for corn and hence no good for hogs and cattle. It took two years for the Midwest farmers to figure that by changing their planting and harvest months a little bit they could get as good crops in the new land as they had in Indiana or Missouri—or better. It is quite true that both the vegetables and beef from these unmulched deserts are virtually flavorless, but the steaks *look* like steaks and the tomatoes *look* like tomatoes. (No California correspondence desired. P.S.)

Now began the great Potato Surplus. During 1848 and some part of 1849, potatoes, usually from Chile, cost anywhere from a dime to a dollar apiece, depending on the latest cargo from Valparaiso—we have seen how the Yankee Trader was badly hit by the inconvenient arrival of a South American boat. But when a cargo of potatoes had been absorbed the price jumped immediately to a dollar a pound or more. So everyone who had a little land near San Francisco had the bright notion of planting some potatoes. The Gold Rush nearly lost out in a race with the Potato Rush.

The virgin soil of California promptly produced a bumper crop and in the season of 1849–50 one could have all the potatoes he wanted if he would promise to carry them off the premises.

The tragic thing about this incident is that during that winter the miners suffered severely from scurvy and cholera. Any dietitian, or any non-dietitian, knows that if the lads had eaten a few raw potatoes from time to time they would have escaped scurvy and probably concomitant cholera. As it was, the sovereign treatment for scurvy was to bury a chap up to his chin and leave him alone for a day or two, as was done to Michael Strogoff, in the Verne novel. Well, ladies still use mud packs. But the antiscorbutic value of raw potatoes seems to have escaped attention for years—it is mentioned in one of Jack London's stories about the Alaska Rush.

The recognized antiscorbutic of the time was the onion. These sold in various seasons for anything from a "bit" to a dollar. (A "bit" was twelve and a half cents and probably derived from the sixpence of early American coinage. "Two bits" is still a common expression, meaning twenty-five cents, which would have been a shilling when the term was new.)

A farmer named Kilburn raised a crop of onions and sold it for eight thousand dollars, using only two acres of his property. This throws some light on the value of advertising. The meek potato was quite as useful against scurvy as the onion but, since it failed to develop a sinister perfume, it was unnoticed; it was years before trade manufacturers began to use the principle of the onion.

John Russell Bartlett, *Personal Narrative of Explorations, etc.*, remarks that people with indications of scurvy instantly sought out the fragrant vegetable and that he, himself, "had eaten them with more relish than he had ever eaten oranges."

It would probably be somewhat difficult for Mr. Bartlett to get the American people to substitute raw onions for orange juice at the breakfast table, but there is much to be said for the assertive onion, doused in wine vinegar with some tarragon salt and black pepper. There is nothing to be said for people who, like this writer, indulge the fancy except that they never have scurvy or engagements for contract bridge, the latter a curse unknown to the miners.

The accounts of the first produce of the California farms are quite incredible to anyone who has not seen the first fruits of fresh fertile territory. A Mr. Frank Page got a shady reputation in St. Louis by remarking that any onion that called itself an onion in California should be about the size of a man's hat-lining band. Under the penalty of laughter he retreated hastily to California; his father followed him there later, saw some onions, and apologized.

It is remarked that most California vegetables are virtually tasteless and that in this cattle country the best restaurants advertise "Kansas City Steaks." The earth gives prodigally of what it has and produces monsters but it has not been mulched by a million years of vegetation, and one does not get succulence from powdered lava, or old sea sands.

There was the inevitable conflict between the quiet farmers and the high-flying miners. The miners considered the farmers clodhoppers, and the farmers thought of the miners simply as bums, which many of them were. This strife did not have quite the features of such conflicts as the Peasant Revolts of the Middle Ages or the pious suicides described in *Karamazov*. These peasants were quite as tough, independent as, and more intelligent than the ordinary gold digger. In fact, the best of the miners intended to become farmers when they had enough dust. No reasonable person intended to swamp around in a creek all the rest of his life. It soon became evident to most of them that they were not going to make a million dollars in six months and retire to Vermont or Ohio as magistrates or deacons, but they did have a possibility of some security at an early age—the median age of the miners was about twenty-five—and the bright ones took ten or twenty thousand dollars and hurried home.

The years between twenty and thirty are precious and no one with a brain in his head wants to spend them picking at gold, mud and lice.

The first warfare was occasioned by cattle. The farmers' rights to their cattle were quite as tenuous as their rights to their boundaries, and poaching a piece of beef was quietly condoned by the early courts. In one early case, where a predator was caught in the act of butchering a steer, the court found that the defendant was not guilty of theft because he had not removed the carcass from the premises. In another, where a fellow was found with a bull's head, justice said that the remainder of the carcass must be produced to furnish a *corpus delicti.*

It is curious that here, a hundred years later, most people think that a *corpus delicti* means the body of the deceased. It does not—it means merely the evidence of a crime, roughly. This is a footnote to the fact that the early courts were miners' courts, that California was slow in realizing that oranges and avocados were its destiny, rather than the pittance of yellow mud the miners dragged from its creek beds and promptly invested in Ohio or Iowa. If California had not had very· fertile soil, all of its gold would never have made it an important member of our comfortable league of nations.

In a country where the best of land titles were very dubious it was necessary only to tear down a fence to show that the land and all the cattle on it were in the public domain. The only trouble was that the settlers were quite as rough as the robbers and a small moo from a kidnaped calf might get one a .45-caliber obituary or a distressing freight of buckshot. In

these decadent times few people know what buckshot is like
—the pellets are about the size of an average pea, cast of soft
lead so that they flatten when they hit anything; with that circumference they naturally expanded and spread when they left
the gun's muzzle, so some of them were likely to hit anything
within fifty yards or so and perform a disembowelment. A great
deal of trash has been written about the revolvers of the "old
West"; not too much attention has been paid to the short-bar-
reled shotgun, which was truly a dreadful weapon, as deadly
in the hands of an amateur as in those of seasoned old brigands.
Even a skip-miss from one of those things was likely to call for
an amputation.

The warfare was never declared; the miners simply stole the
settlers' cattle and the settlers quietly shot them when they
could catch them in the act. The result is in the resolution—
California is now a great agricultural state and its mining is
negligible, except for oil. It was a year or two after the first
fever of the Rush before the quartz miners and their giant
sluices brought the conflict into the open.

Hittell quotes Charles Nordhoff, writing in 1878 of the eleven
months he spent in California in 1847:

"—it was universally believed that but a small part of the
soil would produce crops. Everybody remarked that there were
no trees on the great plains on each side of the San Joaquin
and Sacramento Rivers; and they judged that, as trees did not
grow there, the soil must of course be sterile. . . . He attributed
the ill repute of the state in the early days as an agricultural
region to the fact, in part at least, that the first cultivators
sowed in the same season as in the eastern states and got no
return. But there was a very great and rapid change when people began to understand the peculiarities of the country and
when and how to cultivate and harvest."

Nordhoff then tells of ten eight-horse teams on gang plows
dealing with a forty-thousand-acre wheat field. It is now 108

years too late to discuss the matter, though one is inclined to believe that no California farmer in 1847 had ten gang plows and eighty draft horses. But there is little profit in arguing with a Californian; God once won an argument with Ananias, but California had not been discovered at the time, or there might be some new theology.

The Charles Nordhoff book has the inviting title *California: For Health, Pleasure and Residence.* This had started already.

The issue was fairly settled then, almost as soon as the Gold Rush occurred. Gold was not to be the fortune of this Pacific state; its wealth was in the San Joaquin and Sacramento valleys, and its other estates. After its first brief display the gold turned out to be where it has always been, in the more permanent works of men.

The flumes and sluices brought about the next troubles about what the state thought it was and what it was to be. The miners were guilty of two offenses; they made deviations of creek water for their sluices and they dumped waste gravel on prosperous acres. There must have been some substantial opinion among the farmers that they were the real settlers of California, which was correct, and some feeling among the miners that they were the pioneers, which was not exactly correct because most of them went to the place to grab and go. My own revered ancestor had no notion of settling or developing this dismal land—other people did, and they certainly had the best claim to title. Settlement involves intentions as well as possession; Grandpa was having a brick house built in Iowa while he was digging gold out of California.

It is now somewhat difficult to locate most of the Rush towns of California for the reason that a good many of the original towns were named frivolously or even with a hint of contempt —even loathing. Most residents of Cañon City would not care to have their stationery engraved with the original name of the town, which was Ragged Ass; Ione City once had the simple name of Bedbug. Fiddletown is Oleta.

H. F. Raup surveyed the subject of Gold Rush place names for the *Geographical Review* (quarterly of the American Geographical Society of New York) in the issue of October 1945, considering particularly the three counties, Calaveras, Amador, and Trinity. Most of the early Indian names were revoked at once because Wintun pronunciations were difficult. The two "'lumne" rivers are still so designated but Mr. Raup finds only about 2 per cent of Indian place names in his searches. The Spanish-Mexican names disappeared because the miners did not like Mexicans. Thus the Rio de los Americanos, where gold was first discovered, became simply the American River.

Quoting from Mr. Raup's article: ". . . in each of the three counties half of the original names of settlements are used currently without essential change, though minor variations have occurred in the century since the establishment of the settlements. An example is the name of the town of Murphys, which appeared on maps originally as Murphy's. Successive forms of the name included Murphy's Diggings (1855), Murphy's Camp (1868), Murphy Camp (1888), Murphy (1897), Murphy's (1941), and Murphys (1944)."

Of the thirteen natural features which gave names for settlements or mere guide directions, creeks furnished the most names, followed by bars (river sand bars) and gulches. Bars usually had settlements; creeks and gulches were likely to have more scattered population.

Of what are here called names derived from "cultural features," vastly the greatest number are the names of ranches; these names changed continually with the owners as they still do for farms and properties all over the country, including even buildings used as landmarks. For instance, the Pennsylvania Hotel in New York no longer goes by that name. Settlements, arbitrarily named, are the next in number. In the three counties named there are now mapped 7 of 65 ranch names left from the early plates and maps; of 73 "settlements," 37 have persisted; 2 places are still named for "diggings" and 2 for bridges. The dams, ferries, mills, etc., have disappeared from cartography, except for 8 "unclassified" names for industries or circumstances related more to humanity than nature.

This evanescence of names is possibly illuminating sociologically. In my little county-seat home town, Hangman's Hollow —the place where the sheriff hanged a man before the Gold Rush, the only execution in county history—is still just that, in spite of the fact that the site was filled up and graded for the convenience of Courthouse Hill about a generation ago. Nigger Hill has not seen a colored person for many years, though before the Civil War it had a fair population of useful settlers who came in via Missouri by the famous Underground Railway. If one inquired for my farm in the outskirts, owned by me for only a quarter of a century, he would best ask for the Duffield Farm. Names cling in places where people expect to have grandchildren.

As has been suggested, the miners named their guide points flippantly and even hatefully, and if the settlements persisted, the permanent settlers quickly changed the names. I would, of course, love to furnish my various correspondents with the return address of Bedbug, California, or better, Ragged Ass, but unhappily a wet blanket fell on California nomenclature when people began to go there with a notion of staying, and they seem to have been a little short on pixy humor.

This article remarks that a number of titles were likely to turn up anywhere in the three counties. Big anything (bar, meadow, flat, etc.); racial or national: Dutch, China, Indian, Murphy, Negro, Chile, Buckeye, Kanaka, Arkansas, Italian, Yankee, Beaver, New York, Ohio, Oregon, etc. Jackass was probably instituted by a Missourian—Columbia was named for Columbia, Missouri, and not primarily for the Latin chap who discovered

Watling's Island. Some of these are nostalgic but it is a fair guess that most of them were ironic, intended derogation.

Maybe not. I remember once having had to ask driving directions in a pleasant little Missouri town called Peculiar. Even permanent and dignified Americans cannot be trusted where a small grin is conceivable.

The first agricultural settlers of 1848 and early 1849 seem to have been moderately, though not unanimously lawful. They no more thought of going into California and seizing lands whose owners had proper Mexican titles than a decent person of the present day would think of going to Germany or Japan now and settling on any public land he found apparently unoccupied, though the case is a little different because, with the acquisition of California, the Mexican public lands became American public lands and settlement of such lands was legitimate enough.

The trouble was that in California, with the deluge of 1849–50, the settlers became very careless about what land *belonged* to someone under a Mexican title, and what was actually *occupied*—and the settler-adventurers even became a little more than careless about whether it was occupied or not. Any steer and any land outside a fence was obviously in the American public domain and subject to settlement, in slightly different manners. Also, the ordinary Mexican fences were not very sturdy.

Sutter was probably the greatest victim of the settler ignorance of surveying, decency, and the details of public domain; but there were hundreds of others, particularly the Mexicans, who found great sections of their ranchos and herds of their cattle simply taken from them by similar herds of stupid Yankees who assumed that when the United States had bought the territory it had also bought all private property rights for the public domain.

The squatters sent a memorial to Congress in December,

1849, complaining that they had come out to California to settle the public domain and put it in a state of industry and culture (and they really did make farms blossom on uncultivated
pastures—the culture is a different question) and now found
themselves treated as trespassers.

Millard Fillmore was President at the time, because of the
death of Taylor. He was a Whig but not popular even with his
own party; so he can hardly be criticized even mildly for the
absurd tangle Congress made of the whole California business.
Congress sent out a commission, which it took a year to organize and transport, to straighten out the matter of titles. It
was a commission of three members appointed for three years
(that is, two more than it took them to get there); it was generously allowed four clerks learned in English and Spanish.
This was how California rated with Washington at the moment
—the place dug gold, yes; it was antislavery, the big question
about its admission, yes; it raised oats and cattle—who cared?
What was the fuss about titles for farms? They couldn't ship
the cattle East.

If they had sent twenty commissioners, each with a full staff,
some sense might have come out of the mess, but at the moment if forty commissioners with forty brooms had swept it
half a year, the Carpenter's doubts about getting it clear would
have been more than justified. As it was, the commissioners
were chiefly engaged in determination of the laws, the rights
of tenure of the missions, the body of the law as concerned all
classes. After these things were settled the matters could be
turned over to the courts individually. It was more than a long
generation before the majority of the individual claims were
cleared up. The committee was largely a legislative rather than
executive body.

This would have been all right, but the judiciary of California was not what one could call eminent at the moment; an
appeal from a decision of the commission on the grounds of

their continuing investigations of all the basic titles went to a
court which, if it were competent and honest, had to make decisions on the groundwork largely governed by the determina-
tions of the three heroic men who were struggling in their own
morass of researches and adjudication.

It was an Augean Stable of everything from property law to
international law—the latter being established in its crudest
form at the time—and there apparently was no Hercules among
the commissioners. To render confusion thrice confused, squatters began to squat on squatters. In these circumstances courts
were not valuable and, to paraphrase Napoleon, God was on
the side of the heavier artillery.

As an ethical problem the thing would seem to be insoluble
unless one takes the simple view that the land belonged to the
Indians. Which it did not. There were at least twenty-five
linguistic groups of Indians in California when the white men
came in and, with few exceptions, they were nomads who
moved from place to place and never made a claim on anything as a society. That they were entitled to their unused wilderness is morally correct, on the principle of prior tenancy,
but the claim was not viable because of the fact of abandonment for at least a thousand years of most of the premises.

Beyond that there was the Spanish claim of discovery—the
utterly unsettled Antarctic continent is presently being parti-
tioned by nations that have never seen more than scraps and
spots of it—and the substantial Mexican claim of possession by
conquest and a trifle of settlement. The difference between
claims is evident; in the Antarctic a few penguins had home-
steads as personal property but they, too, were nomadic as the
Indians. However, one could not dismiss the claims of the ran-
cheros as casually and their claims were registered and guar-
anteed by the Treaty of Guadalupe Hidalgo; so if international
morals did not apply here they did not apply anywhere. The
Mexican titles were valid, but the great estates were stolen bit

by bit with the deliberately blind acquiescence of American courts.

A little after the Argonaut days and even during them the cities suffered more from the squatters than did the farmers and honest titleholders. It very quickly became evident that San Francisco and Sacramento were towns of destiny and the influx of squatters, speculators, and dishonest lawyers to these places was a Rush in itself. The government had held Rincon Point as a reserve, but till it got around to using it, it was leased to a Mr. Theodore Shillaber; it took a detail of twenty soldiers to secure him possession. (The carnival and circus term "shillaber," incidentally, was very old before this gentleman's time.)

Bancroft gives a variety of incidents on the squatter wars in San Francisco. One party calmly fenced in a public square and tried to defend his claim with a gun. The famous Captain Folsom repeatedly hired a private army to keep his land clear. There were numbers of small pitched battles, particularly around Mission Street, which the squatters claimed particularly as their own. There were even mildly bloody fights about "water lots," parts of the bay itself which might sometime become valuable for docks or piers; this was a particularly impudent form of poaching, for all of these belonged to the state. Sam Brannan deeded some ground to the Odd Fellows for a cemetery; it was filled with squatters before it could be adequately occupied by its intended population.

In August, 1850, about a dozen people were killed in a miniature war over land in and near Sacramento. In dozens of places the squatters banded themselves together and defied the world, though usually not for long.

The curious thing about this is that while the honest farmers —and there is no irony in this, for there is no doubt that great numbers immigrated under the serious impression that a great part of California was in the public domain—were making this furor, greater squatters with lesser squatters upon their backs to bite 'em, the coarse and ribald miners did very well about property rights. There was claim jumping, of course, but very little of it, because mining had the authority of the various camps. The authority was extra-legal, but it was honest and it was short, sudden, and effective.

They did not even clash with the farmers—for a while.

ELEVEN

Hittell says that quartz mining began in 1850, but this date is much too late; one of the first things that disappeared from Sutter's property was the set of stones that he had obtained for his new mill—the one that brought about the Rush. There could have been only one use for these, detached from a mill, and that was as pounding blocks for quartz, or in the crude sort of mill the Mexicans and Chilenos called an arastra, which was a simple device for raising and dropping a boulder on smaller chunks of quartz till they were pulverized to a size fit for washing, or other processing.

These were followed by larger mills as early as 1850, at least, simply gristmills designed for material larger and harder than corn or wheat. Hydraulic mining, which was expensive and required large personnel, was not important till 1853, some time after anything one could reasonably call the Rush. By this time the rush was to the farms and cities of California and, with the streams and easy placers fairly well exhausted, mining had to go into big business.

The period between Sam Brannan's ride in 1848 and the beginning of winter in 1850 includes most of the dramatic features of the Rush.

The winter of 1849–50 could be called the climax though not the conclusion of the event. It was a bitter, rainy winter and the Fields were largely occupied by miners who were still novices, if not in mining, certainly in the way of life in the region and the conditions. Prices were still fantastic and a good many of the newcomers had not had time to learn the tricks and lay up provision. A majority, probably, of the miners were lousy and all the conditions for epidemics were ideally satisfied. Cholera, starvation, and scurvy were everywhere. It was ironic that a cure for scurvy and an ameliorative for the other diseases lay rotting by the ton two or three days' ride away, down in the orange orchards of the hidalgos and the missions.

As it was, the starvation which weakened men for the other afflictions had only the relief of occasional charity; there were a few tentative and useless nostrums for cholera, and it was only beginning to be suspected that onions prevented scurvy; however, there were no onions.

By the following year things were better, except for cholera. The onion treatment for scurvy seems to have wiped that out, or they may have discovered oranges—there is no further mention of that horrible disease in California history—and there was enough work at the industrialization of mining to keep everyone in beans.

The progress of quartz mining, of the mills and sluices, and the consequent reduction of belated Argonauts to day labor is best illustrated by Rodman Paul's table of wages over this period:

1848	$20 per day for labor.	1852	$6.00
1849	$16	1853	$5.00
1850	$10	1856–58	$3.00
1851	$8.00 or less.*		

* These were undoubtedly summer prices, however, Grandpa Duffield reported in one of his letters that So-and-So, an Iowa acquaintance, offered to work for $5.00 a day, in December, and had no takers at that price. He says the price for an unskilled handyman was $75 a month during the winter—which is not as unfair as it seems because there must have been considerable limits to possible working hours. These estimates must be general and conditional at best.

This steady decline of the wage scale is sadly significant of the fact that the days were ended when even the feeblest soul could expectorate in the boss's eye and go down to the creek and pan a day's wage in an hour. The sands had thinned out and almost any strikes made from now on would be made in the quartz veins, and these were not a one-man or even a small-partnership business.

The United States has managed to produce some of the brightest lights from the briefest candles, in history. For the mines, in their four years or less of adventure, or noisy adventure, made a very profound mark on history. For one thing, California gold furnished a very considerable security for the munitions of the War between the States; it gave the United States and its citizens a gold credit of a billion dollars or so for procurement of materials with which to kill one another. This, however, in the long run, was a relatively minor effect, since people can be killed with crossbows or brickbats as well as bombs, though not as expeditiously.

It took only these two to three years to pan out the easy gold of the streams and turn the region to quartz. Men still panned gold for many years after 1850 and some did it very profitably; the creeks and gulleys were by no means exhausted—they are not exhausted today—but the known rich localities had been thoroughly worked by the end of 1851. When one considers that in some places claims were limited to ten feet on a side, though with unquestioned riparian rights when the claim faced a stream, it is easily imagined how thoroughly this first harvest had been threshed. Except by the Chinese who threshed what had been threshed. They made very good livings from old claims that had been worked two or three times by Caucasian miners and it was generally known that there was no use to bother with a claim that had been worked by one of them. This was one reason why they were particularly disliked and finally riven into the laundry business; they were too patient and careful for the times and manners.

The quartz business had to go into the hands of companies, though that word in its present connotation might be misunderstood; the companies might be four or five men, operators and not mere proprietors, but to handle the quartz profitably took two or more men to get the stuff out, two or three more to pound it up in the mill, and a few more to sluice it and gather the deposit. Later, this grew even more complicated with the great sluices.

In the beginnings, it is true, some individualists smashed their own quartz with hammers and washed it themselves, but this was obviously wasteful. A man could not be procuring his own rock, crushing it, and washing it all at the same time. So the old lone-wolf operation or two-man partnership went down the sluice. This was the beginning of the corporate idea which now operates all of the even mildly important gold mines in the world; it was also the end of the Argonauts. They gradually became prospectors—adventurers, not operators.

With the extension of organization there commenced three conflicts between the agriculturalists of California, to whom the future belonged, and the miners. One was of old standing—mineral rights preceded farming rights and if someone happened to jump a fence and find a promising lead in the middle of a wheat field he could go ahead and work it. Hittell, quoting Shinn (*Mining Camps*), mentions one instance where a whole hay pasture—hay was selling for eighty dollars a ton—was calmly pre-empted by the miners, leaving the owners no recourse, because mining rights came before the proprietorship of lowly farmers.

The legislature of 1852 had firmly stated that anyone with a serious intention of mining could mine anywhere, whether the land had been claimed for farming or not. It was not till 1855, when mining had dropped from $81,000,000 to $55,000,000 and was rapidly on its way down to $17,000,000 that the handwriting on the wall became apparent to the legislators and they made a provision that if any property was damaged in the course of mining, the miner had to pay for it.

In the meanwhile, miners had quietly staked claims on town streets, made whole villages move out of their way and preempted serious settlement with spades. Wheat was never such a king as gold had been in this place. In 1866, because of the sluices and wildcat claims, landowners were finally given exclusory titles to their own property and the rights to the minerals contained. It was not till 1884 that the Supreme Court made mineowners liable for damage to agricultural lands, caused by the dumping of gravel and sand that landed on farm property or choked useful streams. By this time a hundred million cubic yards of sand and gravel had been dumped in the Yuba River, raising its bed drastically in places and destroying, for the time at least, fifteen or twenty thousand acres of the best farm land in the region. Not much, but serious to particular owners.

The end of the Rush meant the beginning of predators—it was a kind of Industrial Revolution in the country. It required a certain time to get California to take its mind off gold—but, then, what Columbus discovered was merely Watling's Island. The quartz mills also brought in entrepreneurs, not at all the Argonaut type. There was a considerable difference between working for wages and delivering stuff to a hopper, and sloughing around for one's self in a creek bed. By 1852 the gallant and lousy days were nearly over.

Over in a way, for the day of dishpans had merely given way to a day of more numerous dishpans of sorts and those are being shuffled to this moment, but in the form of Geiger counters rather than the old tinware. Prospecting. The whole business was taken out of the hands of the speculators by larger speculators, who could wash tons of gravel where the early min-

ers had washed pans, and produce less glittering but less un-
certain gravel from the quartz prospects.

The second quarrel between farmers and miners has been
suggested—the sluices. The third was the ditches by which the
miners diverted water, frequently whole streams, to the convenience of the mills. A farmer who had settled a farm beside a
reasonably dependable small creek and woke up one morning
to find that there was no longer a creek, was less than pleased.
He might, and very frequently did, retaliate by tearing down a
few hundred yards of sluice and using the lumber to fence himself back to water again, or merely to start a good bonfire.
Boards were extremely valuable in the comparatively treeless
Sacramento Valley till the railroads ended mule-train transportation. The mining companies were very sensitive about this
kind of annoyance, but they were no more sensitive than were
the farmers about having ditches cut through their fields and
orchards and their water diverted.

The extent of damage may be inferred from the dimensions
of the Eureka Lake Ditch which was 75 miles long with 190
miles of branches. It had cost about a million dollars; since the
weekly revenue of the chain of mines was about $3000, this
cost would have been profitable if the lodes had lasted a dozen
years, but it is doubtful that most of them lasted even the six
years needed to cover the investment.

And after the '70's when gold production had dropped to
$17,000,000—a trifle then in the economies of California—the
farmers had a superb system of irrigation ditches, some $15,-
000,000 worth, as Hittell estimated in 1897, free of charge. Not
only that, but the sluice dumps, whose gravels were naturally
mixed with a fair amount of topsoil, were found to be quite cul-
tivable. Still, it was not too agreeable for the contemporaries,
who found some of their best bottom acres smothered in apparently hopeless clay and gravel.

The quartz and placer gold was nearly pure gold in most

regions. Along the Stanislaus River it ran about .900. At Butte, California, it was nearly pure and sold at the top rate of $20.40 an ounce. Toward the Sierras it began to be mixed with silver and ran only 60–70 per cent. Hittell estimates the average for the region at .855 which is probably low. Georgia gold averaged .923, what there was of it.

The sluices were merely an extension of what had originally been termed the "Long Tom"—a three-sided trough with baffles at intervals, which interrupted the heaviest of the sand washed through. One baffle would not stop much, of course, but it would flunk some of the freshman quartzites and send them on. At the end of more or fewer baffles; according to the richness of the gravel, all the gold that wished to settle had had its chance.

The miners had known, apparently from the beginning, enough to load the baffles with mercury when they could, to catch the finest gold as an amalgam. The cyanide process, fortunately, was not discovered (by McArthur and Forrest) till the 1890's; otherwise there would be dead miners all over California, since they worked by and large, and that is no way to treat cyanide.

The pre-emption of large territories in the United States is made somewhat more graphic and credible by the tables of J. Arthur Phillips, *Mining and Metallurgy of Gold and Silver* (1867, London):

The following table gives the approximate yields, in lbs. troy, of the principal gold-producing countries at the commencement of the present century, and for the years 1850, 1860, and 1865.

. . . except that the return for California and the neighboring States and Territories for 1865 is probably somewhat under the truth, since it is exceedingly difficult to ascertain the precise yields of Idaho, Montana, Colorado and some other outlying districts.

(It will delight these States and Territories to know that they are outlying districts of California.)

Mr. Phillips' report is that between 1800 and 1850 the world produced about 54,000 pounds of gold, most of it from Asia and Latin America. This is obviously incorrect, carefully speaking, since returns must have been coming in from the Rush for more than a year, but again, carelessly speaking, the yellow dirt may not have been converted into the black ink of Threadneedle Street in that time.

Then between 1850 and 1860 the figures leap to 345,250 pounds, of which about two thirds—not quite—are attributed to California and its "neighboring Territories."

And the casualty occurred. The flock of murderers and petty thieves England had sent to Australia ceased to descend on San Francisco, because they had it in great lumps that would have made the Count of Monte Cristo return to shoe shining. In its noblest decade California had produced, very roughly, 100 tons of gold; in an abrupt exploit, Australia matched and beat it—South Africa and Alaska were after Phillips' publication.

It may be interesting to some prospector to learn that Nova Scotia produced 2072 pounds of gold in 1865. Probably dental fillings from swordfish.

The sluices as well as the ditches became corporate projects; sand was dumped in anywhere along the way and when the baffles were cleaned the whole proceeds went into the company jack pot. The Dutch Flat sluice was over a mile long and must have been fed by dozens of mines and many mills. It is easily seen how the resulting debris could have been troublesome to the farmers who caught the regular effluvium of washed sand and gravel, or found it choking their ordinary water supplies, if these had not already been diverted in favor of the sluiceways.

An unpretentious war was waged between the miners and the farmers. The mining companies, definitely favored by the law, posted sentries about the flumes and sluices, but it would have taken a young army to guard all the points at all times and it took only one leak in the main system to render the rest of it useless. The things kept operating, though, and the final solution in the duel was the very simple one—when the gold gave out the sluices were moved or abandoned.

This usually happened in a brief time. Quartz mining was expensive; it cost ten or twelve dollars to process a ton of crude material—the yield might be anywhere from five to twenty times the cost, but it was not unlimited and gold mining was far from being a permanent investment. The larger companies, with stockholders, had to prospect and move and dig and sluice regularly, and this ate up a good many millions of the millions they could produce.

Today California is third in gold production in the United States, behind South Dakota and Colorado, but during the belated Gold Rush of the 1930's I saw two mines in the Mojave Desert; one was operating on truck-imported water with a "sluice" about the size and shape of a concert harp—the dirt passed from groove to groove till the valuable brown sediment was left in the last one. This was on Ord Mountain; the second mine was in the valley some thirty miles above Lucerne. It operated on deep wells and produced about $2000 a day at a cost of $1200—it could not have been worked profitably except for the sudden decision of the government to set the price of the metal at $35—and then bury it. This matter can be considered somewhat later.

To put a Dickensian postlude on the story, this mass exploitation not only took the individual out of mining but it took the gold out of California. After the bumper year of 1852, $81,000,-000, the output dropped into the $60,000,000's, to the 50's in 1855, the 40's in 1857 and from 1860–65 to 41, 38, 23, 24, 17, where it remained till 1874—which is not part of the Gold Rush story, by a generation.

TWELVE

Owen Wister, or perhaps it was Stewart Edward White, described an early California mining town approximately as: first there was a saloon, and then there was a supply store, and then there were two saloons, and then a lawyer's office and then a saloon and then a doctor's office and then two saloons and then a feed store and then a saloon and then an undertaker and furniture store and then a saloon—I think that's right, stranger, but maybe I forgot some saloons.

(The derogatory use of "saloon" as a drinking saloon has not been found by the Oxford English Dictionary prior to 1852, though there were dancing saloons much earlier, and the substitution of saloon for *salon* was still earlier. The O.E.D.'s first reference on the American saloon as a drinking place is 1884, which is, of course, far too late. Though the use of "saloon" strictly for a rum establishment may be nearly that recent. The general idea was that a saloon was a place of entertainment and dancing seems to have the priority. It will probably shock Roseland and other such respectable dance parlors to know that they are saloons.) (It will probably shock Arthur Murray a great deal more.)

There was a very great difference between the saloons of the camps and the more or less gilded dens of the cities. Since any grocery store in the backlands sold liquor as inevitably as it sold beans or calico, these places did not attain the barroom flavor of the more specialized institutions which could sell one sugar only in the female form and pepper in a faro bank or a roulette wheel. The camp stores encouraged what is called "quiet" drinking, the cups of sociability, and men probably got quite as drunk from a gallon jug as they did from shot glasses in the more specialized parlors of the larger towns, but the atmosphere was not at all the same.

There was little dancing, except some improvised solos, because of the lamentable shortage of ladies, and also because a shop whose principal stock is beans, buckshot, and bacon does not ordinarily engage a dance band. Also, there is a cathedral quality to a general store that cannot be dominated by the fact that a few drunks have intruded on the sanctity of the scales and scoops.

In the larger towns the saloons did not carry groceries; they were places of entertainment solely, and pretended no other occasion. Yet they were seldom the bedlams that are represented in the early sketchings. The first thing that happens to a successful saloon is an attack of decorum. That there were many "dives" goes without saying, but these were as far apart from the elegant saloons the successful miner patronized as the Waldorf is from a "smoke" joint in the Bowery.

The writers of the Rush put considerable emphasis on gambling, which is always an interesting topic, especially to gamblers. Here, again, one has the fallacy of the focus. One supposes that in an ordinary lifetime the ordinary person will bet ten or twenty thousand dollars on possibilities not concerned with the ordinary chances of life, on horses, cards, dice, the outcome of events whose probabilities are not clearly foreseen—like, will it be a boy or a girl—on flipping pennies, on bridge prizes and every kind of trivial occasion. This is hardly called gambling, though it is, when one spends three cents to send an entry to a Non-Stinking Soap contest.

The gambling of the Rush, when it occurred, was concentrated—it rang up noble sums which would have been unnoticed if they had been dissipated over a lifetime. If a man lost a poke in an evening it was noted. If he had lost it in fifty years playing checkers, the horrible game called contract bridge, or mah-jongg, no one would have noticed that there had been any gambling wave at all. Bancroft notes some instances where men lost their hard-earned gold in an evening; this raises the question of what they would have done with it otherwise. Any ass who undertook a practiced gambler would have been quite certain to lose his farm or his grocery store to a banker a little later. And without a possible recoup in the Fields.

There were several favorite games in the region; three-card monte is quite as contemptible as the old Scandinavian game of mustamier, depending solely on chance, when it is honest. Faro is not much better. Black Jack, which the French call vingt-et-un, can be controlled to a very slight degree by mnemonics. Roulette is absurd, even when it is honest. The noble game is poker, where the chances are wide open and the behavior is correct. The "poker face" is probably the highest attainment of man since the Ptolemys, who achieved divinity by mere immobility of expression, as many men have achieved similar greatness in the same manner after drawing a club to four hearts.

Euchre was also a game of skill, a version of what is called "pitch," but one must never forget that all educated card playing is at least three fifths luck; however, the other two fifths can often be the determinative factor. There is an excellent article about probabilities in the Thirteenth Edition of the Encyclopaedia Britannica, and though the professional gamblers were most of a century from access to this splendid work they knew the rules as well as Descartes or Leibnitz in their particular fields. It was ancient knowledge that drawing to an inside straight was sheer folly and that a person had one chance in nine of drawing to a bobtailed flush, under the best circumstances.

There is no report in any of the available documents of any professional gambler cheating in an otherwise honest game. There was plenty of cheating, of course, but not by people who wanted to stay in business. A skillful gambler was like a skillful architect or a skillful dentist. He spent his time at his study and he did not need legerdemain to win; in a roughly mathematical way he knew the chances, and in a roughly psychological way he knew the customers. Gambling was not only a highly technical but a proud profession; most professionals, even if not restrained by fear, would have been ashamed to cheat. There was also the fact that one of the ancient tricks of the business was the "greenhorn" ruse, and a gambler could never be quite certain that the honest, ragged, somewhat liquored old miner sitting across the table from him was not a member of the fraternity and possibly a more educated one.

Bancroft has a whole chapter of incidents on gambling, each pointing a moral; but in his time in America—and in these later Victorian days (1888), pretty much in England—a book that did not point a moral was hardly considered worth publishing. Morals make slow reading. The young miner takes the fortune which he intends to lay at the feet of his loved one in Massachusetts and goes to a wicked saloon for a small fling before he is finally hurled upon the granite bosom of the Presbyterian Church again. He drinks a glass of sinful beer and, naturally, becomes wildly intoxicated—a wonderful money-saving trick if one can achieve it.

Then the young ladies and the gamblers get him and when he wakes up the next morning he has to borrow ten dollars to buy a shovel, a sack of beans, and a piece of sowbelly to start all over again. Bancroft is no more particular about this rake's progress, however, than most of the contemporary writers and the writers of the time of the Rush; indeed the diarists, preachers, and journalists of the Rush write with such vigor about gamblers that it makes one suspect strongly that most of them had been cleaned at one time or another. Any good poker player had about a 40 per cent chance with a reputable professional which leads one to the appalling conclusion that then, as now, about two thirds of the people who tried to play poker did not know how. Hence the prosperity of the gamblers.

Bancroft has one particularly incredible story about the aged Chinese who tossed a bag of coins at a gambler and bet it on the turn of a card. The gambler accepted cheerfully. The Chinese won and the gambler was horribly shocked, when he opened the sack to match it with the pay-off, to find that instead of silver dollars it contained gold eagles—$40,000 worth.

Let us say, for simplicity, that that was about 2000 troy ounces of refined and manufactured gold, or a little less than 150 pounds. The gambler must have been in the last stages of delirium if he did not notice the weight of the bag, and the aged Chinese trotting around with 150 pounds of gold was certainly not Genghis Khan because Genghis was a small man by the best reports. Gold has very nearly twice the weight of silver and anyone pretending to be a gambler who could not tell the difference between 150 pounds of gold and about 80 pounds of silver must have been singularly unperceptive. (The figures are rounded and only approximately accurate.)

There were thieving gamblers, of course, as there are on many ocean liners and main-line trains today, but they were necessarily birds of passage in a place where transportation was difficult and punishments were drastic. There is a considerable difference between changing one's boat to London and changing the route to hell, a populous suburb but with only a one-way terminus. The crooked gamblers were usually amateurs. One of the first hangings in the camps was that of a gambler, identified only as Jim from Botany Bay, whom a blacksmith caught rigging the cards. He would not have been hanged for this—merely flogged and run out of camp, probably—but he added to his indiscretion by shooting and killing the blacksmith.

Within an hour he was as dead as his victim. His trial and execution had some engaging features.

His plea was, "I know damn well I shot him and I know bloody (the epithet gives a good deal of verisimilitude to the story—an American would have thought it was sissy, but an Englishman would have considered it a fine effort) well you'll hang me." He then begged a friend in the crowd for the loan of his revolver so he could shoot a juryman who, he felt, had been markedly unfriendly. The request was firmly refused, but the court did allow him to climb a tree, perch on a branch, adjust the noose, and jump off without urging or assistance.

These Botany Bay convicts, so eagerly unloaded on California by the English authorities, were of the same caliber as their forebears who considered it almost a privilege to be hanged because it gave them a day in the sun and a chance to make a speech, with the certain noisy approval of their old mates in the crowd.

But in spite of their general circumspection the gamblers had one general opinion out against them, "B'iled shirts cover black hearts."

There was also a low opinion of bartenders. They were men with large fingers, because almost the first question a prospective employer asked was, "How much can you raise in a pinch?" When the ordinary price of a drink was a pinch from the customer's dust poke, a good broad thumb was a great asset for a bartender.

What is ordinarily called "vice"—prostitution—is also hardly a part of the Rush story. It belonged almost completely to the towns. It has long been an exploded notion that severe physical labor diminishes desire; if anything, the contrary is true; it would be as silly to say that the hardest working people are the weakest because they wear out their muscles—but there was a stern factor of time involved with the miners; gold was their devoted passion to which they gave every possible working hour.

There was a question of supply, which was quite as stern. Peon women, squaws, and Chilenos were about the only stock available in the early towns; "white" women were almost invariably decent about the camps and were almost revered. This situation changed quickly in even small towns, but working miners had too much work to do to indulge in idle diversions.

There were exceptions. "The Idyll of Rose Bar" would be an amusing title for a sketch on the theme of Goethe's last lines in *Faust*—"Das Ewig-Weibliche zieht uns hinan." (The eternal-feminine draws us upward, roughly.) (The "roughly" is an auctorial apology and does not refer to the manner of drawing upward.)

Rose Bar was a little town in a beautiful location where the Mace family settled in and built a wooden house and planted gardens—the name of the town may have come from their horti-culture. Mr. Mace is poorly described in the accounts easily available; his status is not particularly important except as Mrs. Mace's husband. But Mrs. Mace provided the splendor and the sanctity of a female white woman to the whole Bar, with 199 male persons and one female—also a frame house and roses.

The Bar grew famous, or notorious, for its elegance, which probably includes etiquette, but one can throw that in to complete the specifications. Men shaved every Saturday night and washed themselves and their intimate garments at the same time. (Men have intimate garments, just like women.) Then they went and called on the Maces. The commercial literary societies had not been discovered at this time but Rose Bar would have been a ripe place for the Delphians or what.

Mrs. Mace had a salon with an influence that extended to tidying up the town (in later days, "Clean-Up Day" and "Keep Our City Clean") and sticking a few flowers around the cabins and even getting a little hayseed to make lawns. Rose Bar be-came an oasis of gentility in the middle of a desert of crudity.

Mr. Mace, whatever his position or occupation, seems to have been a gentle soul, up to a point. One day he threw Mrs. Mace out. It may or may not have been because she said defensively that though her husband was a quiet man she could provide enough vice for the whole family. Which she had obviously been doing, since she went to San Francisco with enough money to start a successful "parlor."

What became of Mr. Mace is not known and not important; the important thing is that Rose Bar continued to be a pleasant and genteel settlement, inoculated with courtesies. The local miners never recovered from the memory and manners of Mrs. Mace. And most of them, no doubt, for very good reasons.

This was how ladies were valued in these places. In a way Mrs. Mace's missionary effort was commendable; it softened and modified behaviors in only a small area, but it was a planting point. More conventional missionaries have not been as effective.

Marysville was a fairly small town—a thousand or so, one judges, from the prints available—but it has two curious stories relative to the society of the times. The first has been noted: That the principal society matron was an old settler from the Donner party, therefore somewhat before the Rush, and had dined on people. This made her the Emily Post or Elsa Maxwell of her place, though the latter ladies achieved their eminence by less interesting methods. The second, which is more pertinent, was that by 1851 the Sydney Ducks were sufficiently established in these small towns to kidnap a young orphan of ten or eleven from San Francisco and send her up to Marysville for preliminary training. However the Vigilantes had also been well organized by this time and *one* member volunteered to go up and bring the girl back, which he did by organizing a barroom gang in the town, which made it an unfavorable place for the Ducks to work any further.

For the most part "vice" depended largely on the importations of the Chilenos, Peruvians, and Mexicans in the very early

years—perhaps one should say months, for the Nordic influx
was not far behind the established discovery of gold.

In general the situation was about what it always is; the
biological excitements of the adventure were ameliorated by
the fatigues. Except that these men were nearly all young and
vigorous and the women were unusually predacious, stimu-
lated by the circumstances, there is no reason to believe that
the mines and the whole territory was sexually more "immoral"
then than the world is today.

There is a legend that many of the great families of California derive from the marriages of magnates and madams. It
would be a cesspool job to search the facts—it would also be
tiresome and unprofitable—but one can assume that fewer than
a dozen good California families came from a *mésalliance*—
which may as well have been the mother's as the father's. It
would be equally absurd to say that a few lonesome gentlemen
did not find some sympathies beyond the occasion of the evening, and marry the gals and set them up on Nob Hill a little
later.

"Vice" was probably less extensive at the moment in the
mines than it was in the civilized villages of New York and
Philadelphia, or than it is now in any place in the world. The
men worked all day. But gold put a focus on the vagaries of
California, just as motion pictures do now.

Contrary to general opinion, it is not love that makes the
world go round, unless one gives a wide definition to love. In
this case it happened to be gold, which could obtain any other
love, within limits. There are still people who have particular
devotions above gold. But this was a Rush; a passion of a sort,
and a very jealous one.

THIRTEEN

San Francisco began as Yerba Buena, which is to say, wild mint, or peppermint, which was the name of an island in the harbor, and other settlements on the mainland, but four years or so before the American occupation, the Mexican Alcalde Vallejo gave the town the name of his wife's patron saint, Saint Francis, and this was made formal in January, 1847. The place had 34,000 population in 1850, which made it a very fair city for that time; it was considerably larger than the booming city of Chicago, and larger than the whole District of Columbia.

It was situated as it still is on a range of small mountains, of which a fair number have since been shoveled into the bay to furnish more waterfront and more viability. The two most famous hills remain; Nob Hill, which was settled in the '60's by the new nabobs of the Far West, and Telegraph Hill, settled at a still earlier period—by 1850—entirely by the thugs of the community. It was then called Sydney Town. From here the Ducks emerged at regular intervals to burn down as much as they could of the rest of the town.

For a decade or more after 1850 San Francisco was a completely undigested and indigestible town. In January, 1849, it had three city councils. Its only jail was the dismantled brig *Euphemia*, which lay far enough in the harbor to make escape difficult—premonitory of Alcatraz. In one of the first city elections for sheriff the candidates were Jack Bryant, Democrat, a tavern owner, and John C. Hays, Independent, a former Texas Ranger. Hays would have seemed to be what is now called a

"natural," but the Texas Rangers of that time were not at all
what they have grown to be. They were about the worst gang
of murderous cutthroats in the world.

Bryant, with an enormous campaign fund of spirituous
liquors, would have seemed to have an easy in, and it was so
considered at the time, but on election day Hays appeared on
the streets, splendidly caparisoned in what may or may not
have been a Ranger uniform, putting a fine white horse through
its paces and waving his shiny revolvers. The fickle mob—a
large number of them no doubt more or less drunk on Bryant's
free liquor—gave way to admiration and voted Hays in by a
tremendous majority, possibly not of voters but certainly of
votes.

It was profitable to be sheriff at that time. The sheriff's salary
is not mentioned but the city marshal drew $10,000 a year and
such a salary would have been a minor matter to the sheriff.
What with serving papers, not being able to find people and not
being able to keep his hands on them when he did, closing his
eyes when a good robbery was toward, and a little of this and a
little of that, a law officer could make a very good thing of his
job in early San Francisco.

Even a constable could do well. Two of them were unfortunate—they kept guard while a gang robbed a bank and stole
the safe, which contained $24. The bankers did not trust too
much to their appointed guardians. The thieves and their police assistants then went on and stole another safe, but there
was an alarm by this time and they had to abandon the thing
before they could open it; they also had to abandon $500 worth
of tools.

The city government would have made Tammany Hall
blush for its inefficiency at thieving. The city started out with
sixteen aldermen, each drawing $6000; the mayor, recorder,
city marshal and city attorney each took $10,000, the treasurer
$6000 and the tax collector $18,000—a primary budget of $160,-

ooo, for a town of thirty-five to fifty thousand people. The salaries would not have been too outrageous in the booming town, for the duties would have been onerous if any of the officials had bothered to perform them.

But the salaries were only a beginning. The letting out of contracts for services which were performed shoddily or not at all was the principal business of these magistrates, sales of jobs which in turn were subsidized by every manner of corruption were also remunerative, there were a dozen "gimmicks" by which anyone with the least shadow of authority could share the wealth.

There were a dozen reasons why this state of affairs was tolerated for twenty years and, with brief interruptions of "reform," for many years afterward. The principal reason was that everyone was making a great deal of money and it was not worth while to risk trouble. The second reason, as Bancroft says, was that politically the Californians were preoccupied with national issues and paid very little attention to what was going on under their noses. California has been a very self-conscious state from its admission till the present day, and it intended to have its voice, or yelp, in Washington, and that was much more important than merely having individual pockets picked.

The state had been purchased originally because (1) it seemed cheap on the three-territory deal with Mexico, (2) the slavery forces had had last innings with Texas, and (3) a few members of Congress knew a little bit about the place and suspected that it might eventually be a desirable outlet to the Pacific.

Then, of course, its Cinderella story arose, so that it was admitted to the Union about fifty years before anyone thought it might be, and it was feeling its oats as a full member of a large federation of nations, including such smug places as Boston and Philadelphia.

That it was years before this helter-skelter of population, however large, was moderately fit for even a minimum of self-government, till it could be organized in anything resembling a politically homogeneous population, is obvious. For instance, the South has been traditionally Democratic (Southern Whig), not particularly because of slavery or the wounds of the Civil War (the War between the States), but because the party has always been associated with the jealous protection of cotton and tobacco production. New England has the same feeling about manufactures, and the Midwest formed the habit of voting Republican because its legislators knew they were supposed to keep tariffs down on machines and up on staple foodstuffs. If anyone can trace bipartisanship beyond anything but regional economic advantage, it would be interesting to hear the theory—but not from a platform.

This was not true, of course, in the very early days of the country, when political controversy chiefly concerned the fundamentals of what was still a very tentative government. But in 1850, when California was admitted to the Union, the state had no products to protect—the argument about Florida and California oranges was not present; all of the agricultural products were naturally consumed locally and the population even required supplies from South America and Hawaii, so that the hot political issues had to be Federal. Slavery was the immediate issue in 1850 when California first applied to Congress for statehood and gained it.

The Territory had already had a convention, at Monterey, prohibiting slavery, so that there was a great dither in Congress about California's statehood; there were fifteen slavery and fifteen non-slavery states in the country and California would upset the balance. The Southern Whigs had a majority in the Senate; nevertheless, California was admitted as a free state in 1850; but with a savage Fugitive Slave Act. Also, a proviso that future applicants for statehood could make up their own minds about slavery. The South was evidently optimistic about the settlement of New Mexico and Arizona.

In addition to this exciting topic, Daniel Webster told Austria to go climb a tree when it seemed that Hungary might win its independence; there was trouble with the British in Nicaragua; trouble with Spain over American filibusters in Cuba, and all kinds of Federal and international excitement which California, newly elevated to its junior partnership in the United States and filled with somewhat impulsive people, considered more engaging than the quiet extraction of its back teeth by a lot of petty local swindlers.

The spirit of the times in 1850 was for adventure, in this place. The United States was almost as young as California, as historical time goes—its three quarters of a century very sproutish as compared with England's millennium or so, or Rome's two thousand years. (Rome is supposed to have been founded in 753 B.C. which would give it almost an even twenty-six hundred years over San Francisco, but there are no corporate records. About three hundred years later [390 B.C.] some of my Gaul ancestors tore it up by the roots, but it was hastily rebuilt so that it could be burned again in the time of Nero. San Francisco was burned down regularly in the time of the Rush, but it finally took an earthquake to burn it in modern times, and it was not rebuilt "hastily"—rapidly, but well. Since then no Gaul earthquake has disturbed it much.)

In 1854 Commodore Perry opened up Japan, which would have been a silly thing to do, in the light of more recent events, except that the Russians were about to open it up themselves—both the Russians and Americans had cause to regret their enterprises.

It was seventeen years after the Rush, while America was still licking the wounds of the Civil War, that William Henry Seward, one of the greatest Secretaries of State this country has ever had, bought a thing called variously "Seward's Icebox"

and "Seward's Folly," and got the Russians, who had been such
a headache to Sutter—though no doubt the sentiment was mu-
tual—off the American continent. This was Alaska.

There was gold there, also.

For a total of $37,200,000 the United States bought, consecu-
tively, the Louisiana Purchase, the Southwest, and Alaska; the
Louisiana Purchase included the gold fields of Colorado and
South Dakota and the whole region. As a prospector I would
give you an avuncular relative named Sam. Except that Uncle
Sam was not prospecting for gold—he was merely trying to
make himself secure on a continent; but the son of a gun kept
hitting things every time he pushed a shovel or a plow.

Pretty soon lots of oil and some uranium and such like, but
tons and many tons of the ordinary things to make life good—
bread and beef and nightgowns. And copper and silver and
iron, from Louisiana Purchase, far more valuable in production
than all the gold that has ever been dug. And infinitely more
valuable in use.

In such a melee of national politics and with its first political
whiskers become visible, it is little wonder that California
took a "let-George-do-it" attitude toward immediate affairs;
everyone who had money had lots of money and taxes were
not oppressive. One merely bought a tax collector. Naturally,
the state went bankrupt immediately, and then more and more
bankrupt, but by a Ponzi system it managed to get most urgen-
cies supplied. The richest gold territory in the world, at the
time, was hopelessly busted and no one cared much; the money
went round and round and that it came out in the pockets of a
few fellows who understood the nature of the carrousel was not
too disturbing as long as there was a bit left.

The grand coup of this business was probably the departure
of Henry Meiggs—Honest Harry Meiggs—from San Francisco
on October 6, 1854. This is later than the Rush, but the man's
career falls in the period; how well into the period is not exactly

known but it must have taken him two or three years to steal a million dollars in a comparatively small town.

Honest Harry did a general financial operation as a broker of anything; he loaned money, but the money was forged as scrip receipts from indisputably reputable companies—the California Lumber Co., Wm. Neeley Thompson—and they were given as collateral for loans to Honest Harry's other enterprises and never went into circulation, where they might have been examined. He also borrowed money and furnished the same merchandise as collateral.

There was never any question about his honesty or the value of the notes he supplied, so that they lay peacefully in bank vaults and appeared in transactions merely as credits for this company or the other. He was a power in the board of aldermen and much besought by contractors, for whom he furnished contracts and properly forged wastepaper.

Finally, he fitted out the bark *American*, supplied it with two thousand dollars' worth of liquor and other necessities to match, and sailed out of San Francisco well ahead of the discovery of a note to one of his principal creditors mentioning that he had "failed" for eight hundred thousand dollars. Some writers suggest that his loot was about two million—a million would be a fair guess.

Since he had robbed virtually everyone in San Francisco, the steamer *Victory* put out after the *American* immediately but its engines broke down. At this late date it is impossible to guess what caused the breakdown; it would be cynical to assume that a few gold pieces got into her funnel. Anyway, Meiggs got down to Chile and began building, or financing, railroads for Chile and Peru. Bancroft says that he became an international figure in these enterprises, but one doubts this because of the limited nature of the projects and because someone from San Francisco would certainly have shot him if he had been definitely located. However he did have a career in those parts on his million or two million dollars and what he was able to extract from his new residence. He was very good at extracting and South America was a wonderful place for it at the time. His name is not mentioned in any present history of great fortunes, so presumably his stolen treasure was dissipated when he died, or later.

The California judiciary of those days was apparently not quite so corrupt as the executive government. Quite frequently the references note that some judge or other was not only capable but honest. Such references usually have a brève whistle above them; such judges were so infrequent as to be almost impossible, and the annalists treat them as phenomena. Most of them were subject to bribes or intimidation, or both; very few had any legal education worth mentioning and were at the mercy of semiliterate shysters who had flocked to San Francisco and the mines at the first compelling scent of litigation.

The situation did not fulminate, though, till Sam Brannan and others with substantial properties about the Bay grew tired of the Hounds and the Ducks, robbery, incendiarism and murder, and stopped the business—for the moment—with the plentiful rope around the place. There is still a Brannan Street in the city.

FOURTEEN

It will have been guessed by now that this Sam Brannan, former storekeeper for Sutter, former Mormon who wanted a receipt from God, former hotelkeeper in Sacramento, was quite a character. In San Francisco he went into trade on the grand scale; as far as trade ever pretends to be honest, he was honest; he bought low and sold high—anything, tea, town lots, money; anything.

One of his more notable exploits was the cornering of the tea market. One hardly realizes now how necessary the cup that soothes but not inebriates was to people presently or not more than a generation or two from England, Wales, Scotland, and Ireland. One has only to consider that when George III wished to reduce his seething American colonies to abject submission he put a tax on tea, the one absolute necessity that the colonists could not produce for themselves; and that when George's colonial subjects wished to demonstrate their determination they tossed a cargo of tea into Boston Harbor. (From which it was no doubt fished out by convenient boatmen—a touch of salt improves tea, as the Russians have known for hundreds of years.)

One day when the supply of tea in California was dwindling dangerously, a clipper put in with a whole cargo of tea. The weed was usually quite available because of the trade with Hawaii and, through those islands, with China, but it was in short supply at the moment. Brannan bid in the first lot at the high price of $.61 a pound and then quietly took the whole cargo at the same price. No tea ships put in for some time and

Brannan parceled his purchase to retailers at $1.25 a pound. Mr. Brannan had an eye out for every nickel that seemed to be in danger of growing rusty but he also had great interest in this country of his settlement and plenty of courage to do his part of the job.

The situation of supply and demand was rather unusual in early California, as has been suggested. It had a dependable communication in only one direction—roughly speaking, to the Pacific, and that usually furnished a long route because of the seasonal winds. When eggs sold for $.36 a dozen in the winter season in Boston and possibly $.10 a dozen in Iowa, the prices in California ranged from a half dollar to $1.50 *each*. Potatoes went to $1.50 a pound, prior to the collapse already described, after the Hawaiian supply was exhausted. Supply and demand was so irregular that Bancroft says soberly that a man used bales of tobacco for a cabin foundation. Shortly after that tobacco went to $1.00 a pound, so he tore the house down and sold his foundation. It is not as incredible as it sounds, since, in the small population, shortages and surpluses must have been both drastic and regularly recurrent.

The roll of doctor's prices is slightly less credible. Sixteen dollars for an office consultation; $32 for a visit and an additional $32 for every part of an hour detained; $100 for a night consultation and anywhere from $500 to $1000 for an operation. A general diagnosis and advice cost anywhere from $50 to $100. The night consultation does not seem too extravagant when one considers that the doctor had no Ford and no highway if he had had a Ford, and that he had to carry his surgery and his pharmacopoeia on his shoulders and over his horse. Perhaps it was the horse that charged so much money. And well earned, on a blind California trail in midwinter. Also the cost of drugs and materials and instruments was high. The size of the fee probably saved a good many of the few doctors from riding a night to give some brat a drop of paregoric for a green-apple bellyache. There were also no telephones, so it meant two rides, while the doctor might be unavailable to someone who really needed him.

Most doctors would like to cure a person for the fun of the thing, but they are not unaware that they are the most entreated or solicited—and abused—people in the world.

By March of 1851 there was enough agricultural establishment in California to affect trade very seriously when the place had one of its ordinary droughts. Paradoxically, this was a good sign. One of the most fertile territories in the world had begun to free itself from gold slavery and had begun to work out its evident usefulness. That made no one particularly happy in 1851 when the farms dried up, but it has made a good many millions of people happy in the latest hundred years after the Fields dried up.

In the two years from 1849 to 1851 California went through its roughest period of what one might call assortment or adjustment. It had such casual travelers as would naturally be expected to flutter down at the smell of gold; it had a basically Spanish culture in its foundations; it had the generally lawless and opportunistic scum of four continents. Places like Missouri and Iowa, on the outskirts of America, had a cultural consciousness, while Sacramento changed its socks when the old pair wore out. *N'importe*—it caught up quickly.

It is curious, then, to find California pulling itself up by its bootstraps—and bootstraps is the right word because it had little else to grab at first instance—and becoming a place of arts and universities and wine and oranges—and not too much gold and blather.

The establishment of law in California, recognized and formal law, was almost the latest thing California achieved. The camps were generally well governed by circumstance and rule of thumb—what is called "common law"—but in the so-called cities there were too many people to control by the usual viva

voce of the little camps, and what is improperly called "politics"
rather than "manipulating" took charge of both city and state
governments.

The metropolitan lawlessness of those first few years is described by a dozen writers—except that they attribute it to the
whole region instead of the towns that were large enough to be
lawless. A man could commit a crime and disappear in San
Francisco or Sacramento, but if he committed a felony in Dead
Dog Gulch, population 75, everyone knew who it was, or, if he
happened to be a by-passing stranger, a short conference could
furnish a description of the stranger or his horse as effective as
modern fingerprints. Criminology has developed enormously in
the past century, but every century has had its own methods.
One thinks of Solomon's psychiatric examination in determin-
ing the mother of the disputed infant, or the business of Susannah and the Elders in the Apocrypha.

A peculiarity in a horse's gait might be as good as a Bertillon
index or a bruise showing on a tire track—it depends on what
one has to observe and has learned to observe. And though
there were no telephones in that time, men in a great hurry
could spread communications by relays of horses—as in its most
spectacular instance, by the Pony Express—with almost incredible speed in every direction.

In the unorganized and inchoate cities the situation very
quickly grew intolerable, but the intolerability was not particularly noticed till the business of the places came to such a
substance that outlawry was offensive.

One's first glimpse at the early history of San Francisco, for
instance, is a glimpse into a criminal chaos. There was a con-
stabulary of sorts, but it was about as effective as that of London
at the time of the Bow Street Runners. It had many judges who
lived on fees and bribes. As in London of the 1600's, the honest
citizen's best protection was a good gun and a good eye.

San Franciscans did depend on guns in a small way but they

were nearly helpless against the ragamuffins of Market Street and Telegraph Hill (later so named) who could burn up half the little clapboard town to distract attention while they looted the other half. This is an exaggeration, possibly, because they usually burned only a quarter of the town but they sometimes did better than half. But from 1850, with a brief interval, till 1854, no one who owned a wooden building in San Francisco ever slept well abed of nights. Citizens were subject to raids, arson, daylight attacks without a pretense of police intervention, extortion and such simple mayhem as the Ducks and the knife carriers could conduct quickly—ears, eyes, etc.

The Hounds were formed primarily as a social secret society, Bancroft believes, by the New York volunteers who had been shipped to California for the American occupation during the Mexican War. There is probably well-founded opinion that these volunteers were sent to the peaceful shores of the Pacific because no commanding officer in the field wanted any part of them—they had had enough trouble shooting and hanging Irish deserters and big-city looters as it was.

There is considerable difference of opinion about the original usefulness or original criminality of the Hounds; it would seem fair to say that the "protection" the Hounds sold in 1848 and early 1849 was often worth what it cost. After that it became candidly what "protection" is in big cities today, and that took place in so few months that what services the Hounds may have rendered, in the absence of anything remotely resembling an effective police force, may have been neglected. Or they may have been "protection" blackmailers from the first. Both attitudes have a certain amount of justification; from the obvious character of the original Hounds, probably the New York volunteers, it seems quite certain that there would have been a mild amount of felony from the moment these uninjured heroes organized, and it is reasonably certain that in six months they were swaggering, bullying, blackmailing or threatening scoundrels.

There is, of course, no way to compute the size of the organization. *Some* of the New York volunteers must have been decent and gone to the mines or into trades, but anyone who was racially blond and had ten dollars could join the outfit. It was a Ku Klux Klan and we have them with us always. And they all turn out about the same—Hitler, Peròn, Stalin, Mao—and it could have been Andrew Jackson or an even later President, except that the United States is very diversified and born to independence.

The ease with which the fellows were finally put down leads one to believe that they were more ubiquitous than numerous and that their power was built more on noise and violence than on any overwhelmingly extensive membership. There was one instance where a protesting merchant was told to shut his mouth about the seizure of some goods or the robber would bring forty of "the Boys" and tear his shop apart. A gang of forty would hardly terrorize a modern town of thirty thousand or so.

"The Boys" indicates the New York origins of the gang as does the name of their clubhouse, the Tent of Tammany. This name had not accumulated much of the stench that it acquired in 1860 under Tweed but it was by no means perfumed even in Gold Rush days. Early in 1849 the Tammany Boys noticed that "Hounds" was an unattractive name so they changed it to "Regulators." However, to the public in general they remained Hounds or Boys. They collected tribute from merchants and householders; the sheriff, C. J. Pullis, was also steward of the society. He used the Boys to collect debts and serve papers for him, on a percentage basis, when the going threatened to be a little rough or the claim was dubious.

The curious thing about these Hounds was that they frequently behaved in the manner which is unjustly attributed to one of the better animals in all zoology. They could scent a sheriff's commission farther than a fox could run but they also sucked eggs on the side, which is a death warrant for real hounds.

Simple overconfidence destroyed the Regulators early in the days of the Rush. They might have plundered quietly for a year or two but on Sunday, July 15, 1849, they started a full-scale riot that could not be disregarded. Their leader was a fellow named Sam Roberts and on this particular Sunday, in a fit of drunkenness or in attempting to work off a hangover, Sam decided to drive all the Chilenos out of San Francisco.

This was not such a bad idea as it might seem from this distance in time; as has been mentioned, the Chileno district was a stench even to the hairy and calloused nostrils of the early San Franciscans. If there had been due process of law, most of the scoundrels whom the respectable citizens of Chile had been glad to unload on California would have been returned on the first boat. But the place was highly deficient in immigration laws—there weren't any and no one to enforce them if there had been. The unwritten immigration laws had been in effect since the beginning of the Rush but they had naturally been somewhat haphazard, with a few deportations to Chile, Mexico, China, and Heaven.

The frequent references to "Chilenos" is, naturally, a libel against the Pacific pioneers of the New World. Probably every Latin American from Guatemala to Tierra del Fuego was called a Chileno, for various reasons, the principal one being that few anthropologists visited the mines and it was simplest to establish a categorical term. There must have been a considerable population of immigrants from Peru, northern South America and Central America, but it was easiest to call them all Chilenos. There may have been some jealousy of an older culture—the "Chilenos" had been trained miners for two or three centuries; also, our Yankee Trader particularly noticed the pretty girls of the Pacific ports.

As it may have been, the "Chilenos," with the Indians, Mexicans and Chinese, came in for the particular dislike of the so-
called Celts and Nordics of the country. The dislike may have
been justified in some measure, for the Chilenos, like the Ducks,
seem to have aggregated in particularly disreputable groups.

This may as well be told the way Bancroft tells it—he was a
great researcher with many assistants—but deleting such matters as "Circe, the bright-haired daughter of the Sun, in her
enchanted isle of Aeaea amidst her fawning spell-softened
wolves and lions, was not more treacherously lovely when with
her wand she changed the companions of Ulysses into swine,
than was audacious roguery, lapped by flush California, to
the brainless adventurer."

"On the Sunday afternoon mentioned [July 15, 1849], at
about one o'clock, the Regulators paraded in full force, with
drum, fife and banner, and epauletted officers. There were
about one hundred of them. . . .

"Their intention was now none other than to drive all Span-
ish-Americans from the city as they had been driven from the
mines and the final blow was to be struck that afternoon or
evening.

"Sam Roberts commanded and it was noticed that he was
more than usually grave in his demeanor. . . . Supper was
taken at a restaurant, where an eye witness says that Sam behaved badly . . . and to give more forcible expression to his
order for a gin-cocktail appetizer, he kicked over a table and
broke a few glasses. The company then proceeded to get up
steam for the grand assault. This was accomplished by entering
various saloons and demanding drink and cigars; if not instantly
and cheerfully produced, the rioters would go behind the bar,
help themselves and their associates, then smash a few decant-
ers and mirrors as an admonition. . . ."

[A considerable passage referring to Bacchus, Caesar and
the fear of God.]

"Sam drank sparingly that day; the potations of his men he sought to regulate according to their several capabilities. The time having arrived, armed with pistols, knives and clubs, and filled with patriotic enthusiasm and liquid fire, they filed off and marched rapidly down the street to the Chileno quarter. In answer to the question, 'What are you going to do?' they unhesitatingly replied, 'We are going to whip and drive every damn Chileno out of town.'

"Rousing with blasphemous yells and pistol shots the peaceful inhabitants of this then somewhat remote vicinity, they attacked the unoffending [sic—the general opinion is that the Chileno settlement was a blot of thieving and whoring; they certainly were not miners or otherwise gainfully employed] foreigners as they crawled from their dwellings. . . ."

Apparently the Chilenos also ran saloons in their shacks and tents; the Regulators took one of these over, beat the proprietor, drank up or smashed the stock, and then destroyed the tent.

This went on all afternoon and evening with depredations by separated gangs of Regulators on anything they found to despoil. The destruction of the Chileno settlement was probably not as important as the swagger—for a little time they had taken over the town and ravished it, defied it. Anyone could have told Sam Roberts that it was not a good idea to step on the toes of the Californians. The loot of the Regulators had gone down to Tammany headquarters, but Sam Roberts was not present to participate; he was out encouraging the bands of Regulators.

On Monday morning it occurred to the solid citizens, the merchants and bankers, that if the Regulators could run wild over the Chilenos and the saloons of the town they might easily take over trade of all kinds.

The imperdurable Sam Brannan appeared on a barrel on Monday and suggested that the citizens should regulate the Regulators. The crowd was sympathetic, so that when persons in the mob flourished revolvers he dared them to shoot him. This was not as heroic as it sounds, since every thug in the mob knew that if he took a shot at Brannan he would be killed the next instant.

Brannan removed himself from the barrel to the roof of the one-story building occupied by the alcalde, Mr. Leavenworth —his name is still unpleasantly alive in Kansas—where he appointed committees to hunt the Hounds.

Isaac Bluxome had the job of finding Sam Roberts.

Bluxome went to Roberts' address and found that his man was not there; he had pitched a tent somewhere on the Presidio road but he was not there, either. In the meanwhile Tammany Hall was invaded "and several of the gang taken prisoners."

With two hundred and thirty (230) volunteer police on their trails, the members of this gang which had terrorized San Francisco for six months or more scattered promptly. Seventeen were arrested on the ship *Warren*. The great Roberts was dug out of the hold of the schooner *Mary*, bound for Stockton, where he no doubt intended to reassemble his gang.

The prisoners were put to trial on Wednesday. Roberts promptly "proved" an alibi by two parties who said they had seen him to bed before the riots. Nevertheless he was found guilty, along with the others, and sentenced to ten years in any penitentiary the governor might find available.

The governor (Peter H. Burnett) could not find a penitentiary available for the excellent reason that there were no penitentiaries; so some of the prisoners were shipped away and the less culpable were discharged. A good many of the Regulators fled to the mines, where they immediately learned that camp justice was far less complicated and more drastic than the brand dealt out in the cities.

The whole episode of the Regulators was a comparatively brief one and the purging of the gang took place almost entirely between a Monday and the following Wednesday; but it was vitally important as an example of what a citizenry, with no law worth mentioning, no police and many corrupt courts, could manage through the simplest organization. Nevertheless, crime was barely singed by the elimination of the Regulators. The ineffable Sydney Ducks still clung to their quarter and still tried to burn down the town regularly, sometimes two or three times a night. The Regulators who had been freed or had not been apprehended had been conditioned to the idea of bullying and still demanded free liquor, free food, free clothing, free everything.

These were not as easy to obtain now, however. A man ran a good deal of risk when he tried to take goods by simple confiscation; one of these pseudo-communists, who attempted to walk out of a store with a shirt and other articles of clothing, was set upon by the other customers and nearly cudgeled to death before he was turned in to the sheriff. In the good old Hound days no one would have dared to lay a finger on the fellow and the merchant would not have wanted anyone to do so. The community was bored with the whole business; everyone was very busy, and when people are fully occupied with personal affairs the memory of small public incidents does not last long; still, the San Francisco public had indicated that it was capable of reprisals, and this was enough for the Hounds.

After the end of the Hounds, popular law enforcement lapsed. In the first place, a very small percentage of the original settlers expected to stay in California more than a few years and had none of the sense of pioneer establishment that accompanied the settlement of the Midwest. When they had their money they would go back East, even if that East was only as far as Iowa or Missouri—there they would take a real interest in legislation and magistracy, but not in the affairs of this orphan territory. In the second place, everyone was too busy to bother with injuries that did not directly concern him; the tempo of the place naturally induced a selfish indifference which could be disturbed only by such major outrages as those of the Hounds.

The major outrages were not long in coming. Lulled by their triumph, the good citizens let things go much as they had gone, and there developed rapidly scores of small gangs—a pack of jackals to follow where the wolf had been. It would be more or less in the moralistic style of Bancroft to suggest that similar opportunism makes most of the rotten spots in a democracy. Someone else may add such obvious aphorisms as that negligence is actually a kind of corruption.

While these affairs occurred in San Francisco the outlying and remote towns did not escape without harm, but their vulgar —in the best sense of the word—and immediate processes of law discouraged outlawry and nearly prohibited gang crime. These lads were busy with their mines, they had no courts or jails, so they went to the simple resources mentioned earlier. Since they had no more penal resources than San Francisco they either beat the devil out of thieves and threw them out, or hanged more serious offenders forthwith. They had no facilities for the entertainment of legal delicacies, and no time, and no appetite. A two-hour trial was sufficient, followed by immediate execution of what was usually a considered verdict. The classical case, both by its nature and by precedence is that of Placerville. Again we quote Bancroft, omitting classical comparisons and theology:

"To Placerville belongs the honor of the first popular tribunal of the placer-mining epoch. Distant but nine miles from Coloma, where gold was first discovered, the spot where now stands the town was early occupied by diggers. . . ."

["Hangtown" was virtually the port of entry for overlanders who had just crossed the Sierras.]

"Placerville, however, was not the original name of the camp. It was first called Dry Diggings; afterward, for the reason which we shall presently see, Hangtown.

". . . Five men, one night about the middle of January, 1849, had entered the sleeping-room of a Mexican gambler named Lopez, and had attempted to rob him. One of them had placed a pistol at the head of the gambler, while the others seized his effects. Before they could escape Lopez had succeeded in giving the alarm. Roused by his cries the miners had rushed in and seized the whole gang.

"Again, I ask, what could they do? Stand there holding the thieves, until a jail was built, or until Congress should send sheriff and judge? . . .

"So they selected from among their number twelve, who ordered the culprits to receive each thirty-nine lashes; which having been well laid on, with due energy and decorum, three of the five, Garcia and Bissi, Frenchmen, and Manuel, a Chileno, were further charged with robbery and attempted murder on the Stanislaus the autumn previous. The charge was easily enough proved; the men, lying exhausted from their late punishment, were unable to stand or speak during this second trial. (What shall be done with them?) the improvised judge asked of the two hundred assembled."

The answer was fairly obvious. "Hang them."

"E. Gould Buffum was there and begged them in the name of God, humanity, and law, to desist from their meditated [sic] action."

It would be interesting to trace the antecedents and career of E. Gould Buffum but it is not particularly apropos. In spite of his interjection, the prisoners were "bad men and this thing must be stopped at once."

There is a beautiful nursery simplicity in this verdict. They were "bad men" so in the span of fifteen minutes they were, as De Coster says in the magnificent *Thyl Ulenspiegel,* "strange fruit blossoming from a tree."

This immediacy of judgment and execution was not as impulsive as it sounds. The miners did not enjoy hanging people, the preparations and disposals were very troublesome for decent people who had unremitted works at their small quarries; but in a lawless territory they simply figured that "bad men— must be stopped at once." My grandfather saw one hanging in his two and a bit more years south of Sonora, and the event was sufficiently exceptional to be mentioned in his journal. There were few outright lynchings, if any, and certainly no burnings at the stake or such amusements as the Nazis enjoyed; the idea was simply to get rid of incorrigibles without any mess.

And so life went on in the camps, and criminals usually avoided them. To be a stranger, who was not actually digging, put one under suspicion at first instance; this was realized by passers-by. Small places were and still are too intimate for persistent wrongdoing. They are even too intimate for survival; within my lifetime, in this century, I have seen families moving out of Iowa for Kansas or Texas because chickens or hogs turned up as Lost Persons too often in their vicinity. There was no question of violence; it was simply suggested that the parties move out and that was about the way things happened in California. In cases of violence punishment was more drastic.

These simple dramas were played out quite successfully in the multitude of small camps about the gulches of the Rush. They flogged and exiled or hanged a man now and then, though not nearly so many as motion pictures or television would have one believe, and lived quite peacefully. There is absolutely no evidence that any of these people were ever haunted by the fact that they had liberated a squamous soul from a disagreeable body. They were protecting themselves and that was that.

It was quite different in the cities, which had neither the casual society of the camps nor the ill-organized efforts toward a society. With a pretense of law the cities were more assaulted than protected; the courts were corrupt, the police were contemptible; a good gun was the only insurance.

Four of the first five state governors of California were named

"John"—one might as well say five of the first six since Milton
Latham who interrupted the "John" succession was governor
only six days—at any rate Johns ran the place for twelve years,
with the unimportant interruption mentioned, so that the citizens of California promptly fixed the name of "I, John" on any
person who happened to occupy the office, the words being
the first two of any gubernatorial ukase, of course. "I, John"
was the ruler of the state in its first dozen critical years and "I,
John" was generally held in contempt and disregarded by local
justice.

McDougall and Bigler (John, in each case) were the more
notorious of the governors; they never let a vote go to waste on
the end of a rope for the slight reason that the constituent happened to be a murderer. Bigler was the more resounding scoundrel of the two—he probably caused the death of a good many
criminals not really in the capital class, because the miners hurried to execute sentence before Bigler's inevitable pardon could
arrive.

The case of Hamilton McCauley is typical of the local operations. McCauley was a southerner who had not realized that
California was a free state; he took a casual poke at a Negro
and the colored person beat him up thoroughly, a commendable action.

Though California was a free state, there were considerable
differences of opinion about slavery and Negro rights. Benicia
was a southern town and the neighboring village of Napa was
northern. McCauley managed an argument with a man named
Sellers about slavery and Sellers mentioned the beating Mc-
Cauley had just taken from a free colored man. This was intolerable to a chivalrous southerner, accustomed to striking
when he could not be struck back, so McCauley stabbed Sellers
fatally—more chivalry.

There was a good deal of feeling that McCauley should
be hanged without any further diversion, but they finally man-

aged to try the fellow. On the day before the execution the citizens of Benicia got a reprieve from the governor. However, the man who ran the ferry was not feeling well that day and the sheriff was also indisposed and anxious to get his duties done; so that when the party from Benicia arrived it found McCauley stretching a rope.

There was not so much political dissension as this incident would indicate. Everyone was too busy with gold and trade. The colored people were mildly timid about their new freedom and, since the southerners were not too highly regarded by the predominant free-state people in the mines, everyone thought that it was as well to let the issues which were moving the United States into a Civil War be disregarded for the time being. Besides, the Chilenos, Mexicans, and Chinese furnished enough whipping boys. In fairness to the miners, they did get a very poor selection of those peoples, but a good one would not have pleased the first settlers from New England and the Mississippian West.

A Chinese, for instance, could not take a Bible oath; they wrote his name on a paper and burned it to attract the attention of his ancestors to him and his veracity. Bancroft guesses that they lied about as often as Christians; that is, whenever it seemed advisable.

The triumph over the Hounds was more or less a Pyrrhic victory. As every law officer knows, a government of crime can finally be exterminated by starting the excision at headquarters and working to the cancerous extensions. It is much easier to work the problem inductively than deductively, to work from a cortex outward rather than to try to trace a specimen to the central cell. The great coups of modern gangster history in Chicago, Detroit, New York, and Brooklyn have occurred, not when some insignificant little mobster has been executed, but when some big fellow has been sent to the electric chair or Florida or Italy.

But in this case after a successful first step the citizens did not follow up.

With the disappearance of the Hounds, individualistic gangsters had no further fear of stepping on toes. Every doctor knows the danger of dissipating an infection in the effort to exterminate it. So the cities of California were probably more lawless after the disbanding of the Hounds than they had been before. They had changed an army for guerrilla bands.

Historically, these things were almost incredibly immediate. It was only about six months between the dispersion of the Regulators and the founding of the Vigilantes. Good old Sam Brannan—the same guy who would pay tithes only if God gave him a receipt—was conspicuously active in regulating the Regulators and in forming the Vigilantes. By this time he had his finger in every pot boiling west of the Rockies.

The beginning of the end in San Francisco, which was the beginning of the end all through the region, was the Burdue-Stuart business. Paradoxically, crime was more effectively discouraged by the fact that a man was not hanged than by the fact that any number of men had been, indiscriminately. Briefly, the tormented population very nearly mobbed and executed a completely innocent fellow who turned out to be nearly the double of a badly wanted outlaw. The occasion sobered the outraged citizens and led to the institution of mob courts which were at least as conservative as and definitely more honest than the legally appointed courts.

This was the inception, if not the historical beginnings of the Vigilantes.

Stuart was a fairly well-known outlaw of the time; he was being hunted for the murder of the sheriff of Auburn and for a variety of crimes. On the evening of January 19, 1851, a person went into the general store of C. J. Jansen & Co. in San Francisco and asked to look at some blankets. He was shortly joined by another person—they were both covered with whiskers, which was not unusual, and wore peaked hats drawn well down over their faces. They then attempted to kick Mr. Jansen to death and took two thousand dollars from his cashbox. It was a piddling attempt, as Samuel Taylor Coleridge, "Fine Art of Murder," would have testified. When one robs a man and then attempts to kill him, the best thing to do is to see that the victim is dead. Mr. Jansen was not and recovered to identify his murderers. He was doubtful about them at first, then more certain, and finally positive. The interesting thing is that he was quite wrong. The persons he identified were quite decent ordinary citizens.

The prisoners were in a very bad position, however. Crowds surrounded their places of detention, suggesting with some firmness that everything could be settled by merely hanging the prisoners. Fortunately the authorities managed to delay this procedure.

And then they found Stuart. Burdue so closely resembled the man that a dozen people had sworn in good faith that it was Stuart; but it happened to be Burdue. Mr. Burdue missed hanging by less than one day.

Possibly this is a good case for moles on the nose and strawberry marks.

Oddly enough, or perhaps not too oddly, these near slips of justice encouraged crime rather than acting as a deterrent. If Justice could nod once it could nod again, more profoundly. A whole plague of shysters settled on the courts of the California towns and practiced an ancient stratagem—delaying a trial till no one cared much about it and, in this itinerant population, the witnesses had disappeared. So there were two types of justice in the place—that of the camps where a criminal was given fifteen minutes for prayer, and that of the cities where a murderer might be only briefly incommoded by his lawyer's fees.

The Vigilantes did not come about as a revolution or any explosive measure. The winter and spring of 1851 developed

so many cases of murder, assault, robbery, and incendiarism
that the businessmen of San Francisco organized a patrol of
about one hundred men, twelve on duty at a time, for eight
of the night hours. This system was highly reminiscent of the
"courts of summary jurisdiction"—what we now call police
courts—which were only about twenty years old in England,
a considerably older country than California. These police had
power only to detain and the method was unsatisfactory from
both ends. A completely innocent citizen might be detained
on the suspicions of a completely inexperienced officer; a very
guilty one might be dismissed for want of evidence other than
that of the arresting officer. The plan was inadequate, particularly as this extralegal force was confronted by corrupt courts
and such legal talents as those of Hall McAllister and other
scoundrels who used legality to controvert law.

The determination to constitute a separate executive and
judiciary branch was not easily taken—it might not have been
taken at all except for the distance of California from Washington. California was by no means a united nation—years after
the first impulses of the Rush, southern California discussed
separation and union with the South, or, if not that, the establishment of a separate republic. What they were going to establish it with is problematical—possibly Los Angeles, but if
that had happened, most of Oklahoma and Nebraska would
now be paying town taxes. The United States was or were
rather indifferent to this Territory except as a source of gold.

From the first organization of the band of watchmen there
was talk of a permanent extragovernmental society to protect
the merchants and peaceful society of San Francisco and its
region. Two of the principal citizens, James Neall and George
Oakes, had a conference on Sunday, June 8, 1851; its result
was the usual one—they had better talk to Sam Brannan.

This redoubtable character never conferred with anyone except as chairman of the board and any grass that grew under

his feet was badly scorched on its first appearance. With Neall and Oakes, Sam drew up a list of "trustworthy"—meaning both morally and physically—citizens to be on hand at the California (Fire) Engine House *the next day* at noon. Brannan had a lifetime policy of if 'twere done 'twere best done right now, dating at least from the time he whooped down the streets of San Francisco announcing the discovery of gold on the American River, and from the time when he demanded a signed receipt from heaven. He is possibly not what one could call a noble figure—merely magnificent. A kind of Ajax in action, but a good deal smarter than the Telamonian lad.

One can say conservatively that the movement was popular. On Tuesday a Mr. A. Delano drew up articles for the forming of a "Committee of Safety"—human nature being what it is even at its best, it must have given Sam some pleasure to tell Mr. Delano that he was a day late. He liked to be there fustest with the mostest, and from Sutter's fort to his "rooms" in San Francisco where he was able to accommodate a gathering of two hundred people, three years after chopping plug tobacco and weighing beans over at his store in Sutter's, was a considerable hop.

There was some argument about the name of the new society—"Regulators" was discarded at once because it still smelled of Hounds; "Secret Committee" had some fragrance of things like the Lion's Mouth and the Blue Chamber or the Inquisition—these people wanted to act publicly, outside the law, but lawfully. The consideration they gave their name commands respect; "Committee of Vigilance" meant nothing more in the way of police authority than any citizen possesses —to be alert and oppose wrongdoing.

There was nothing extralegal about this, of course; every citizen is supposed to be observant for violations of law and has a duty to prevent a crime or detain a criminal—though in detention he had better be certain about the criminal. But from the first the Committee of Vigilance never had the slightest notion of restricting its actions to these ordinary civil duties; the judiciary was corrupt and anyone who voted the Democratic ticket had only to wait for his pardon to come from McDougall or Bigler, the succeeding governor, who, by government within the ordinary definition, could have made the Committee unnecessary.

The constitution of June 9, 1851, is marked by the economy of its statements—in a time when most public statements usually ran to a considerable amount of verbiage. The specific provisions regard the physical establishment of the Committee, its personnel, its intentions—"perform every lawful act for the maintenance of law and order." This was amusing, since they immediately defied the law in the interests of order.

The "bylaws" had more viscera. Paragraph One says simply that they are out to get people who steal, rob, and burn, since the police "by carelessness or connivance" don't manage the job. And that every person of suspected or known criminal associations should "leave this port within five days from this date."

Article Three, that a committee of thirty persons look over immigrants and reship them to their countries of origin if their credentials were doubtful.

Such a regulation two years earlier would have saved all the trouble. Such a regulation adopted at the same time by the whole country would have saved the United States an almost incredible amount of trouble, which it still endures.

The brave words and resolutions were instantly put to the test.

FIFTEEN

The Assembly Hall was the Fire House, which had a large bell; all members were pledged to hurry to the place at two taps (later three) of the gong. The bell was not long in sounding, only a few hours.

Most of the merchants and agents of San Francisco, accustomed to the security of the good old days (two years old, but by 1854 veterans of the Rush were publishing their memoirs), kept their securities in safes that were amenable to a rap from anything larger than a tack hammer. Some of these kept as much as fifty thousand dollars in dust, for shipping, in safes that could almost have been kicked open.

A shipping agent named Virgin—what a trial that name must have been!—had such a strongbox; one day while he was out on the wharf watching one of his boats sail, having left his office door unlocked as usual, a chap who called himself John Jenkins, actually named Simpton, picked up the safe, dropped it into a boat, and started across the harbor.

Virgin returned immediately and missed his safe. Plenty of people had seen the man row away with it but did not know it was stolen. A boat posse instantly started out after the man and caught him well out from shore. Jenkins promptly threw the safe overboard, possibly to lighten ship and more probably to detain his pursuers, but there were enough of them to handle the two tasks of recovering the safe and continuing the pursuit at the same time. The safe was recovered; in the meanwhile the experienced boatmen of the San Francisco waterfront quickly overtook Jenkins and enthusiastically offered to shoot him if he offered the least resistance. He surrendered.

Ashore, some policemen turned up, without oars, and offered to take charge of the prisoner. They were rudely told to go get some prisoners of their own and not try to take other peoples'. The first meeting at Brannan's had not yet dispersed when they were told that the new Committee now had a suitable specimen to work on.

Then the Fire Company's bell rang and it was time for all good men to go to the aid of the party. Probably the greater part of the crowd that rushed there went to see what new attempt was being made to burn down the town, but a hundred or so knew what the measured taps meant. One supposes that most of these must have thought that it was a test, for it must have seemed a little too soon and appropriate to have a serious occasion for the services of even the most vigilant Vigilantes.

However they all turned out and learned, certainly with excitement and probably with some pleasure, that the Committee was so promptly to have a testing of a serious sort.

The organization would make or break itself on its conduct of this affair and its stoutness in inflicting whatever penalty it might assess. The whole town turned out, of course; the Vigilantes for business, the decent citizens in alarm, and the criminal element to find out where the fire was so that it could assist in the looting. Speakers from the Committee immediately told the crowd that there was no fire—that a new Committee to enforce order in the city, headed by Sam Brannan, whom every person in the crowd knew by reputation, had captured a robber red-handed and now intended to try him and punish him if he were found guilty.

It was a startling new idea, but probably anyone in the audience would have bet two to one that nothing much would happen to Jenkins, though he was a well-known scoundrel. That a lawyer would get him out or that he would bribe a jailer and escape would have been the ordinary procedure and it would finally be followed in spite of the unauthorized Committee.

The prisoner was even more certain of this conclusion than the crowd. Bancroft describes him in the words of an eyewitness as "Rough, tall, powerful, of fine physique . . . he stood glaring defiance through the dim candle-light. . . ." He was an English convict up from Sydney and he had no slightest doubt that he would either be rescued by his pals or taken by the more generous law within minutes.

One of the unfortunate things about these Ducks was that if they had had the stamina to reach Sydney from London and then become sufficiently troublesome to be released on America, they were likely to be the toughest of the breed.

The Executive Committee immediately organized as a court; naturally the great Sam Brannan was the judge, with all the members of the Committee as assistant judges; this, probably, to save the time of selecting a jury. Now, the sergeant at arms cleared the court of "all save the members and officers of the tribunal," which is to say, all who were not Vigilantes.

Since Jenkins' latest crime was notorious, there remained the question of how much this instance was aggravated by the general character of the defendant. A deputation was sent out to find witnesses in his favor, but for once no one appeared with an alibi or a eulogium. On the other hand, there were a number of people present very willing to testify that he was an habitual and arrogant criminal.

Even so, when it became apparent that the accumulating evidence was going to lead to a capital sentence some of the members of the Committee began to show signs of wavering; none of them was drunk and most of them went to church.

Whereupon rose a party named William A. Howard, laid his revolver upon the table, and said firmly, "Gentlemen, as I understand it, we are here to hang somebody."

The trial went on three or four hours, till eleven o'clock, when the prisoner was taken out of court and the "jury," consisting of the whole body, was called to render a decision. The decision was, of course, "Guilty" and the penalty assigned was hanging. The question of when the execution was to take place was equally simple—immediately, before the ruffian element could stir up a riot and an attempt at rescue.

Ryckman (Gerritt W., out of Albany in 1849) went to the prisoner and told him of the decision of the court.

Jenkins was quite as certain as the crowd outside that the sentence would never be executed and received the announcement with the simple comment "Bosh."

"Mr. Jenkins, you are to die before daybreak."

"No, I am not."

"Any money or message for your friends?"

"No." As a matter of fact he had $218 but he intended to spend it himself.

"Can I do anything for you?"

"Yes. Give me some brandy and a cigar."

These were furnished and he went at them with enthusiasm. It was suggested that he might want spiritual consolation and this seemed a good idea to him and after some consideration he decided that an Episcopalian minister would be as good as any. Not only was he amused by the idea of a minister, particularly as he was not going to be hanged at all, but the performance would give more time for his friends to rally.

A Reverend Mr. Mines—appropriate name for a preacher in the place—was summoned and went in to the sinner. Time passed and the Vigilantes grew increasingly impatient. Whether the preacher was carried away by an access of enthusiasm about rescuing a lost sheep, or whether he believed that the proposed execution was a lynching and deliberately delayed matters is doubtful, but most people would incline to the latter idea, since the reverend gentleman got nothing for his prayers but curses.

By and by Ryckman had had enough. He went into the room and said, "Mr. Mines, you have now consumed forty-five minutes and I want you to bring this prayer business to an end. I am going to hang this man in fifteen minutes."

In the meanwhile it was thought best to test the temper of the crowd outside, to learn the nature of the resistance that might be anticipated on the march to the gallows, so-called. The job of haranguing the multitude fell to Sam Brannan, as did all dirty jobs because he loved them. Unfortunately, there was no shorthand reporter present to record this effort which was spoken of with awe by people who heard it, thirty years later. He cursed the courts, the lawyers, the judges, the police, and taunted the citizens with their submission to the rule of crime. Finally he reported that the prisoner had had a fair trial and would be hanged on the plaza in one hour. Sam's vocabulary could be quite blue.

He then asked if the action of the Committee was approved by the crowd. The response favored the "Ayes" but there was a substantial vote of "Nay." The lawyers, headed by a chap named Broderick, the police, and the criminal element were against the hanging, naturally, the legal gentlemen and the police because a deal of this sort didn't make them a cent, and the ruffians because they were literally opposed to punishment in general. These were the three parties with whom the Vigilantes must contend in getting the prisoner from the hall to the rope.

But the Committee had friends outside who had rigged up two heavy ropes as an aisle for their procession. The Vigilantes moved out two by two, with the bound prisoner under heavy guard, and with Mr. Bluxome's assurance that if anything like a successful attempt were made to rescue him, he would immediately have his head blown off. It was at about this time that Jenkins knew that this was it, but the observers did not notice that it affected him. Undoubtedly he had never supposed that he would die of old age.

There was a small incident at the plaza when the crowd thought Jenkins was to be hanged from the flagpole and protested this use of the same elevation which flew the American flag during the day. The people were assured that this was not the plan and subsided.

The chief of police, Benjamin Ray, made a token gesture at seizing the prisoner and was brushed aside. The criminals did little more; there was a grimness to the procession and such evidence of stern organization that it cowed the mere mobsters. Broderick and his anti-Vigilante partisans apparently never made an appearance.

The Committee had rigged a pulley and a rope from the veranda of the old customs building and at about two-thirty the noose was placed about Jenkins' neck. Brannan commanded all good citizens to lay hold, which they did—or at least as many as there was room for—with such energy that Jenkins, still smoking a cigar, had his neck neatly broken. The body was left under guard till six o'clock the next morning when it was turned over to the city marshal.

The coroner's jury determined that John Jenkins came to his death by strangulation, which was not true, and singled out nine members of the Committee, including Brannan, as persons "implicated by direct testimony." The Committee's reply was that it was unfair to single out so few persons and offered a document signed by 180 persons saying they also were implicated.

As the great Burke said, one cannot indict a community.

Also, in the few days following the execution more than five hundred of the most respectable citizens of the town applied for membership. No judge, however venal, no shyster, no rigged jury could have handled eight hundred of the best citizens of San Francisco.

The movement swept through the countryside much more rapidly than that of the Regulators or the forays of the Ducks. The Committee quickly decided that prevention was simpler than hanging and set up a kind of immigration bureau which examined passengers and promptly returned undesirables to their native places—usually the eastern cities or Australia. Hundreds of informations poured into the Committee. The police suddenly became unco' friendly because they knew they were as much under observation as the criminals; the courts and juries knew that a few members of the Committee were attending the more egregious trials.

A great relief sighed through California—that is, lawful California. The Committee offered a five-thousand-dollar reward for the apprehension of any arsonist with the evidence against him, and thereafter it was not safe for a fellow to burn up part of the town—his own pals might have a covetous feeling about that amount of money. In fact, it was not very safe for a poor cove to do anything in the way of a little dishonest profit, for the Vigilantes had quickly accumulated an extensive dossier on every known scoundrel in the city—the Committee went even farther and watched every movement of unrecorded persons who behaved suspiciously.

The slightest variation from rectitude might bring the dreaded message:

"You are warned to leave the city within five days. The Committee of Vigilance. No. 67, Secretary."

The command was not arbitrary. Anyone who wanted a trial could have one, but the existence of the dreaded dossier was known, and most of the warned persons left—and went to some small-big town, though not to Sacramento, which had an effective Committee closely in touch with San Francisco. They went to Stockton or Marysville or Sonora, where the authority of the Vigilantes was still dubious.

If the warned party did not leave or ask for trial he was quite certain to find himself on a boat bound for New York, Sydney, or Peru or some other place of origin, and most of them had very good reasons for not wanting to revisit those places. With a considerable export and a sternly supervised importation, San Francisco soon found itself comparatively free of crime, an astounding but pleasant new condition, for the first time in its American history.

The Committee had its headaches; the criminal element managed to introduce members and it was not easy to weed them out as it is never easy to detect counterespionage that is moderately skillful. Very little attempt at secrecy was made, particularly in the matter of trials and decisions; everyone in San Francisco knew who the principal members were, but in the ranks identities were preserved by numbers, since a majority of the members had to work as plain-clothes men. There was, naturally, a password for the meetings—there is also one for military camps and boundaries where the assembly is too large to give a possibility of visual identification. The Vigilantes were as susceptible to espionage as any other body engaged in serious business, and unwilling to admit intruders. But there was no hocus-pocus; no masks or robes or grand hailing signs— in a membership of over eight hundred at least half of the members must have concealed their identities from each other by the mere fact of non-acquaintance.

The other difficulty was that false notices to vacate began to appear. The Chinese, particularly, were early to appreciate the possibility of getting rivals in business or members of other tongs back to the Orient. But it was not limited to the Chinese. If the Vigilantes had had some bank-note paper with proper engraving on which to issue warnings they could have coped with this easily, but all they could do in the circumstances was to deny the warning and attempt to find the forger.

But there is the old story—twenty presumably honest men in Paris received messages, "Fly! All is discovered!" And the next morning nineteen were gone and the other was packing. Which, minus a little exaggeration, was about the way these false warnings worked. The Vigilantes never wished to be terrorists and they did all they could but in the nature of things no one will ever know how effectively—how many persons quietly stole away without saying anything to the Committee.

The Committee had other troubles. They had small internecine disagreements—Sam Brannan himself had a quarrel with the sergeant at arms and resigned all his offices. Sam was a wonderful executive but possibly not so good as an administrator. He was strong for direct action, without any of the frills which actually kept the Vigilantes in public respect. But his methods got the Committee its *first* respect.

Another annoyance was the Broderick party. David C. Broderick, later a United States senator, was the ordinary politician of the time. He was the son of a stonemason who took him from Washington to New York in his youth. Later the young Broderick ran a saloon, joined a fire-engine company, and became an accomplished ward heeler. Why he went to California when such a promising career offered itself in New York is a matter of speculation—he could have been as corrupt in New York as in California, with like success.

It distressed him to see a possible client hanged, just as it distressed the shysters of the time and place to see judgments executed without any possibility of obtaining a fee. Broderick managed to organize a meeting of these people and their shivering clients, and thereafter occurred a deluge of verbosity between the ward heeler's cohorts and the newspapers, to whom Broderick was repulsive, mixed with a series of legal actions against the Vigilantes and pronouncements by the venal and absurd governor, John McDougall. (Broderick was belatedly killed in a duel in 1859, too late for this account.)

McDougall could have given no more encouragement to the Vigilantes than he did by pardoning notorious criminals right and left on the one hand, while he wrote denunciations of the Vigilantes with the other. To all denunciations the Committee made no reply whatever; it simply continued to function, and most criminals would rather have had a remand from the Committee than a pardon from the governor, for obvious reasons— a remand from the Committee would give a man time to get out of town; a pardon from the governor left the fellow at the mercy of the Vigilantes.

The personal intervention of the governor did not save two confessed bandit-murderers, called, but not named, Whittaker and McKenzie. Whittaker had made a lengthy confession to the Committee of a whole series of crimes and the coincidental evidence was such that there was no doubt of the truth of his statement. So he and his partner were to be hanged. But the success of the Committee had been such that the watch placed over the men was slack and the sheriff, with a posse, was able to seize them and place them in the new jail, still only partly roofed.

The good governor came down from his heights, at that time in Stockton, and uttered statements about due process of law. He did not appear much personally, and Sam Brannan and the rest must have sneered at some length. This McDougall played it both ways from the middle; most politicians then were elected by the ward-heeling tactics of people like Broderick and Ward McAllister, but there was a power above the politicos and that was the men who controlled the money. For by large and minor larcenies, early California was continually in actual, if undeclared, insolvency. The richest gold country in the world was always bankrupt.

So McDougall had to step softly. One day he would offer a manifesto against illegal administration of justice and the next he would congratulate the Vigilantes on cleaning up the premises. He could make reference to one statement or the other as convenience required. In this case, with the law upheld and the prisoners safely in the hoosegow (a word deriving from the Mexican *juzgado*—tribunal), he was emboldened to speak out for due process of law again.

Every idiot in San Francisco knew that if the two men were tried, Whittaker would deny his confession as being obtained under unlawful duress and there was not much other evidence. The sheriff's triumph in gaining custody of the prisoners made the Vigilantes or Vigilants, who had failed in vigilance, more red-faced than they had ever been before in their history.

The amusing thing is that the sheriff obviously had no appetite for the whole business. He had had to make a show for the governor but now the show was over; the Committee did nine tenths of his work for him, far better than he could have done it, and he wanted to keep it friendly and co-operative.

Bluxome was sent to see what armament the jail had and was admitted. By some simple devices he learned that the spare arms in the jail were kept unloaded. Ryckman went to confirm this and found that the old flintlocks were indeed unloaded.

"We don't want any trouble with you," said the jailer who admitted him.

"A lot of people feel the same way," said Ryckman.

Ryckman went to Whittaker's cell and Whittaker permitted himself a grin.

"I hope you are not sorry to see me here, Mr. Ryckman?"

Meaning that he had escaped from the Vigilantes and his dismissal was only a matter of a little routine.

Ryckman was annoyed. "Sir . . . you were tried and convicted by the people; you escaped, but you will as surely be executed by the people as you now live. Entertain no hope otherwise. Be ready. No power on earth shall save you."

(This dialogue on the authority of Bancroft. However, it gives the effect.)

On Sunday, just after services, the Vigilantes rushed the

building as the prisoners were dispersing from their rites. The resistance of the guards was tentative; they knew that it was poor policy to annoy a Vigilante. All of the guards were covered by the "large pistol" of James B. Huie. The prisoners were hustled out and thrust into a carriage which took them to the headquarters of the Committee.

The constitution of the prison invites curiosity when all of the guards could be covered by one man with a "large gun." The only conclusion to which one can come is that the officials respected the authority of the Vigilantes much more than they did that of the governor, so-called. A meager idea for regular government but useful in this place.

At the Engine House they were hanged without benefit of clergy, immediately. They had had plenty of clergy on their conviction by the Committee, before the escape—escape to the sheriff; then followed by recovery by their executioners. Report from the officer:

"Agreeable to your orders above, I detailed thirty (30) men, who proceeded in three divisions . . . and in the short space of five minutes from the first charge the prisoners above named were on their way to your headquarters. J. W. Cartwright."

Ten minutes later the prisoners were deader than ducks. They had already been condemned by the Vigilantes, so there was no use to waste time. The gallows were prepared and there was no delay.

In any dubious case the Committee simply did the detective work and turned the culprit over to the law. In this way, Mr. T. Belcher Kay, an undoubted incendiary and looter, was discharged by a court and escaped to the East. It is not unreasonable that the Committee resorted to the execution of its own verdicts, but there are no records that indicate that the Committee of 1851 accomplished more than four hangings. Those were enough; after that the Ducks and the other rats made at least a pretense of having honest employment. The Committee had to be revived in 1856, when the mines had generally gone into large production, but that is not part of the story of the Rush.

SIXTEEN

The fancy, or exploit, or enterprise did not die without a struggle. The seaways and trails to California were thronged for several years after the proper "Rush," but there was a considerably smaller percentage of miners. The sands of the place had been sifted in an amazingly short time and the hysteria over fortunes to be won with a shovel and a dishpan had subsided; big business had been enforced by the necessity for shafts, sluices, crushers and, even this early—1852—sometimes hydraulic apparatus.

However, the new substantial establishment of California offered new opportunities for birds of all feathers, from prostitutes, gamblers and politicians—a descending scale—to professional men and women, from curates to carpenters. Miss Edith Magoon has recently presented the diaries of her grandfather, George D. Magoon, to the Iowa State Historical Society, which has published the Rush sections of them in its Quarterly *Journal of History*, April, 1956, very pleasantly edited—which is to say, without violence to Mr. Magoon's ideas of spelling, grammar, navigation, or anything else, by an associate editor, Miss Mildred Throne, whose footnotes are a fair history of the occasions in themselves, a splendid job of editing.*

Mr. Magoon was born in Massachusetts, generally a dismal place, in 1825. He arrived in Muscatine, Iowa, a splendid place, in 1840, and in 1847 "took up" the carpenter's trade. "Took up" is a deceiving phrase; it sounds as if he had begun the art at

*Hence I am about to steal quite a lot of it.

the advanced age of twenty-two; actually, it meant that he was
sufficiently advanced to "take up" the trade—as a professional,
not a pupil.

In those days—and it is still true to this day in many places—
a carpenter meant the whole gamut from contractor to architect to builder to cabinetmaker—and to interior decorator and
engineer. They were the Compleat wise men when anything
was to build. The square rule is not a symbol of Masonry, which
probably derived from the Renaissance, for nothing.

Five years later Magoon decided to go to California. There is
no suggestion of any financial distress in this decision; he and
"a group of men" decided to "try their luck in California." He
was twenty-seven, but he was five years beyond the completion
of his training in a trade which was always employable almost
anywhere. Even today we have "tramp" printers, mechanics,
newspapermen—even cooks and tailors—sufficiently skilled to
be secure wherever they land briefly, and keen "for to see and
to observe" before they are trapped by age or marriage. The
efficient Germans used to work this out of their youth with a
"Wanderjahr," but these practice flights are older than history.

Before Mr. Magoon was through with his expedition to
Golconda, in fact almost as soon as it began, he had good reason to be glad that he was a "carpenter."

Mr. Magoon started out from Muscatine (a place since cele-
brated for its use of the bellowing river clam in the manufac-
ture of "pearl" buttons) on February 9, 1852. The notes on his
travels to New York indicate that he was in no fever to reach
the gold fields; the family pilgrimage from Massachusetts had
left friends and relatives scattered all over the country, from
Keokuk through Ohio to New Jersey and New York. At Erie
he and his companions connected with a train and they made
New York City on March 1.

There they paused to see "Barnum's" Museum, which "has
everything that you could wish to mention"; Magoon also saw

Edwin Forrest in *Richard III* and Mrs. Forrest, "a fine looking woman and a good actress," "the trinity Church—a most splendid building" and various plays. No Rush here.

They left New York on March 5 and made Nicaragua nine days later. He then spent eleven days at a hotel in San Juan del Norte. On April 3 they reached San Juan del Sur on the Pacific. Here this leisurely Rush ceased to be fun and sights.

"This is one of the most god forsaken towns in the world . . . what surprised me most was to see the same preacher that preached to us on the steamer a few weeks before tending the bar at one of the gambling houses."

He then spent a week entertaining fever. When the ship *Monumental City*, which was supposed to complete the terms of their tickets, arrived it could take only four hundred of the crowd, leaving about one thousand. The *Pacific* would take only its own passengers, so the thousand were left to their devices—some of them started back to New York and some of them died.

After three weeks Magoon "took a job of work." "We have to go to work or starve." However, employment was no problem. The funds of these joyous playgoers had evidently reached the bottom of the barrel, three months out of Iowa. They should easily have been in California by the terms of their tickets, but tickets were sold in those days when cardboard was available, rather than ships.

By May 8 they resigned themselves to taking a "sailer" rather than the prescribed steamer, and put off for California on the *C.I. Dow*. From then till July 15 they had the ordinary hardships of a sailing voyage, as well known to the Phoenicians and Magellan as to them, since sailing is sailing, through the ages. They had disease, short rations—though Magoon remarks that the sea was full of fish—a ration of water—though any child could have made a distillation apparatus out of a few bottles

and tubes—and the usual dissensions with the captain about
all affairs.

Mr. Magoon was now about five months from Muscatine; he
would have done much better to go from Muscatine to St. Louis
(which he did), then by boat to Independence, and from there
by stage to either San Francisco or Sacramento, since there
were stage routes to both points in 1852. This would have saved
him about three months and simplified his odyssey almost to
the point of boredom—which is no doubt why this young Iowa
Yankee decided to do it the hard way and joined the Marines.

In 1852 the trip to California was no longer extremely ardu-
ous unless one chose to make it so. Miss Throne remarks the
expedition in travel between the various united states between
Mr. Magoon's trip out (166 days) and his return in 1854, two
years later (32 days), by the same (sic) route. He came back
by Panama, not Nicaragua.

If Mr. Magoon had really been in a hurry to reach the gold
fields, rather than in indulging himself in a commendable effort to see some sights before he settled down he would have
taken the Independence stage route mentioned. And if he
wanted the sea trip he could have made the easy ride from
Muscatine to Chicago and then traveled by boat and *railroad*
to almost any point from Chicago to Washington or Portland,
Maine. (Historical Atlas, American Geographical Society,
"Railroads in Operation," December 1850, p. 139.)

This was the same kind of Rush voyage that Ulysses had
to explain to Penelope. Mr. Ulysses wanted to see things, so it
took him eight years and, fortunately, a thousand lies to explain his delay over a trip that would have taken a week in a
good canoe.

Mr. Magoon wanted to see the country and some old friends
and relatives, so he made his circuitous trip to St. Louis, up
the Ohio, and so on and so on. If he had been "Rushing" he
could have thought of five better ways to do it. Even in 1852

there was no longer any hurry. Picking up chunks of gold in stream beds was already a passé notion.

As well as anything this signifies the end of the Rush. The passion or desperation to get there first was all gone. There was still gold there, yes, but it was not to be had for the plucking—and the harvesting was not so exigent.

Postscriptum, one must conclude Magoon. The gentleman really did get the gold fever, perhaps by a sense of smell, and he refused hospitality in San Francisco—anyone from Ohio, a brief residence for the young Magoon in his childhood, has relatives everywhere, including Borneo, where some cousin is a missionary—and went on to Sacramento and from there to Marysville, already mentioned, and toward a place called Foster's Bar. They were carried fifteen miles and then had to walk ten miles and arrived with "sore feet and awfully fatigued." This hardly seems to be the stuff of heroes—but he was a '52er rather than a '49er. The next day they marched the remaining fifteen miles under full pack and were "so near used up we have to lay by a day or two."

This chronicle of suffering is irresistibly reminiscent of the Yankee Trader, previously cited, who had no LUCK. Fifteen miles is not much walking for a day unless most of it is steeply up hill. After three days the hero was sufficiently recovered to go to work on a flume at $7.00 a day. On Thursday he had blisters; on Saturday he received his pay and on Sunday he started for Downieville. At places he went "over some verry high mountains and dangerous places where if the mule should of sliped we would go down over rocks hundreds of feet."

It apparently did not occur to this rugged pioneer that he might have gotten off the mule and trusted his own feet. However, his feet do not seem to have been too reliable. On Monday the little company, apparently five of them, set to work at sinking a shaft. On Tuesday they washed some dirt and got about $2.00, $.40 each, about an eighth or ninth of an ounce.

However, it was not the amount but the presence of "color" that counted. This was on July 27. Three days later they were down 26 feet, where they began to hit "watter," boulders and "cement"—that is, shale so hard that it was virtually soft stone. On August 2 they struck a ledge of rock and also some damp —gas—which had to be blown out. Also, Magoon had been intermittently sick ever since Nicaragua—malaria, most probably —and he had another attack.

On Wednesday, August 4, he and Dr. Nelson "went up the river to work for the Pitsburg flooming Company at one hundred dollars per Month." He reports that the company was taking out four or five hundred dollars a day. They lasted a week on this job, probably at carpentry, since the "flooms" needed constant repair, particularly when they dumped their waste gravel on farmers' oat fields. The interesting thing about this is that skilled labor had dropped from about $20 to about $4.00 a day in the Fields in three years, as is noted—approximately —earlier. The year before my grandfather had paid $10 a day for relatively unskilled labor.

Back at the mine they found that their partners had taken out $16 in the latest two days. The day following "the four of us took out of the Bar $17." The next half day, Friday the thirteenth, they took another $8.00 and went to town for grub.

Then there were engineering difficulties with boulders and watter, but one week later they struck a vein of "rotten quarts" (broken quartz). For about a week things went very well, $10, $17, $22.25 (how they weighed that $.25 one will never know—it would have been a pinhead or so), $16, $15, and $6.00 before going to town on Saturday.

This was not bad, late in 1852, especially as there was always one or another of the partners off making wages at some other job. And by 1852 the prices of staple commodities had dropped tremendously from the fantastic prices of 1849. In fact, the partners were so elated by their prospects that they decided to build a cabin—a cabin with "Claboards" and shingles and "births"—which they did in the remarkable time of six days. They hauled and laid up their logs in two days—in spite of their sore feet and blisters and fevers, these lads had nothing wrong with their arms and shoulders.

"Sunday 19th I went to town and bought some plates nives and forks I thought as we now lived in a house we must do as people do that lives in houses

"Monday 20th I made a door table and some stools

"Wednesday 22nd I compleated our Cabin today and we are going to have a house warming tonight Doc went to town and got two kinds of liquor we had amongst our guests a live yankee from Main we all made it up to get him drunk but I am ashamed to say that we finally succeeded but not till we had all had a little to much."

A "live yankee" seems to have been notable to this child of Massachusetts, such is the absorptive genius of Iowa, but the great state of Maine, foremost in Prohibition efforts since the beginning of the United States, may well take a bow for this outnumbered Mainer or Mainian who rendered the conspirators' victory merely Pyrrhic.

However, there is something to be said for the conspirators. The next day they dug and timbered six feet and started a wing dam. On Sunday Magoon made a "Coffin for a man across the plains." This is sufficiently cryptic but not as much so as the entry for the following Sunday.

"Oct. 3 I went to town I sold out my interest in the Muscatine Drift Co to the Co for $200 the reasons for doing so I shall not state here"

On Monday he bought into a partnership which had an eighty-foot shaft. The first day of this arrangement the new company dug $2.00. For a week things were not much better, but then began days of $15 or better—on Thursday, the four-

teenth, they took $28; the fifteenth, $67; Saturday, the six-
teenth, $48—and they declared a dividend of $34 and left $23
for running expenses with the treasurer. In the following week
they made $64, $40, $38, $43, *$152*—and then $7.00. They had
to start a new drift and made nothing of consequence for a
week. However, in the meanwhile, Magoon saw a mule fall off
a mountain and attended a Masonic Lodge meeting. Then they
resumed profitable operations for more than a week—on Saturday, the twentieth, they took out $272—the best day on Mr.
Magoon's record.

A week and a day later, for no apparent reason, he sold out
his share in the partnership to his old Muscatine partners and
started for Sacramento. Winter was coming in, of course, and
a considerable number of the miners were starting south, but
it hardly seems sufficient reason for selling out at $100—a claim
which paid the company $272 in one day and $96 two days
later.

The most reasonable conclusion is that Magoon was tired of
mining life in one of the worst winters of early mine history.
At any rate, he went to Sacramento City where his services as
a carpenter were at a premium in a town which was growing
out of the winter mud almost miraculously. There he worked
steadily on various buildings; he saw three men hanged; he
saw Lola Montez, etc., etc.

There is an amusing account of a balloon ascension on Sep-
tember 4, 1853:

". . . they sent up a baloon with a boy in it but did not give
him any instructions how to let off the gass [It is interesting that
Mr. Magoon could spell "instructions" impeccably but could
not spell "gass."] he kept going up till he likeed to frose and
as he passed through the clouds a couple came in contact with
the baloon and broke it [These were California clouds. Author.]
which caused it to come down in a hurry so fast that it nearly
took his breath so soon as he struck the ground it began to

ascend again when his weight was off he tried to hold it till it carried him some 11 feet up again when he let the tarnal thing go as soon as they found that the baloon boy had got back there was an awful shouting the boy had his adventures printed and is making lots of money out of it the first day he sold over $300 worth he is considered some of a hero

"Sunday Nov 6 . . . I am very lonely today and thinking the time is short for my stay in California. . . ."

He did his last day's work in California exactly two months later, January 6, 1854—two years, within a month, after he had left Muscatine. He left San Francisco for Panama—which had returned to favor as a transcontinental route during his expedition—on a steamer which took 7 days to reach Panama, rather than the 47 he had spent on the "sailer" from Nicaragua.

He reached home without further important adventure and became an important contractor and builder in Muscatine.

There are two obscurities in this account. In one place the diarist says that now was the time to go home because the fare from San Francisco to New York was only $15. But he paid $100 to go to Panama. This may have been the difference between deck and cabin fare.

When he "disolved" his partnership in Marysville he found that his net profit from his mining, above the expenses of two years, was $1155.38. But since he had spent a number of the later months at carpentry, he probably reached Muscatine with what was, for the time, a fairly substantial bit of money—and with a great deal of experience. He lived to seventy-five (d. 1900), so the Muscatine doctors apparently knew how to deal with California fevers.

SEVENTEEN

By 1852 the miners had scooped out about all of the easily available gold in the creeks. The East had settled down; the Mexicans, Chinese, and Chilenos had learned that their vicissitudes in the Territory would not be limited simply to those of mining, but the end point was that large companies had gone into the business of vast excavation, if one can call it that, since it was chiefly done by washing down hillsides or sluicing out whole acres.

As was the case in many other kinds of mining, notably iron, the tailings, handled massively, proved much more productive than the original fat deposits. Eighteen fifty-two was the best year the mines had with over $81,000,000 but for two years the figure stuck close to $70,000,000 before it began the melancholy decline which ended with $17,000,000 and stuck there. At present the biggest gold mine in the country, as was mentioned, is at Lead, South Dakota, and there they dig virtually pure blue clay, but with a tiny content of gold which makes the great operation profitable. An individual miner would not be able to dig $.10 a day. In the Mojave Desert, forty miles or so from Lucerne, they were operating mines in 1933 whose yield was about $2.00 a ton—the interest and depreciation on great installations and the cost of driving five wells would have been fantastic for a '49er.

At the same time, the agricultural influx was rapidly changing the character of the country. When the farmers belatedly got mineral rights to their orchards and fields the destinies of

California were set in a proper direction. The *annual* crop production of California is now between two and a half and three billion dollars a year; even making a differentiation for the values of money, this is a great deal more value than was dug from the mines in the five years which generously include the Rush.

EIGHTEEN

The good of it was as fantastic as the project. It scared the living daylights out of every treasurer in every bank and government in Europe. The United States had a favorable position in trade, with cotton, tobacco, indigo, some foodstuffs, a few manufactures, whale oil, lumber and minor products. It was not really dependent on Europe for anything essential, though such things as pepper and silk and tea made life more agreeable— but the cusses were getting the stuff from the Pacific, now, and they were also building up a gold account that threatened the whole establishment of European finance.

This was not a new headache for the old world. In 1568 Jean Bodin, in his *Reply to the Paradoxes of Malestroit,* announced that high prices were due to the introduction of gold into Europe from various sources (probably the New World and Africa) and it is amusing to hear his complaint echoed three hundred years later by Sir David Barbour, *The Influence of the Gold Supply on Prices and Profits.* He might as well have reprinted Bodin. J. P. Booth, *Gold: A Delusion,* reiterates the dismay about oversupply of the token.

The primary effect of the Rush was to establish the United States in the world with illimitable credits; America apparently had enough barter tokens to buy anything. When Holland threatened to go on a silver standard the United States promptly discovered more silver than had ever been in the world. This was a noble opportunity for Russia, which was coining easily malleable platinum into small coins worth a penny or thereabouts—and Russia had all the platinum there was at the time. However, who gave a damn about platinum?

To coin money now out of uranium would probably make the average householder uneasy, besides, the pure metal would not last. That is the value of gold as a barter coin.

There is a stupidly simple solution to the whole thing. The values of services and products attain a general level, no matter whether you are using tokens of gold or wampum.

The United States now has about twenty-two billion dollars in gold in its reserves, of which only slightly more than half is held at Fort Knox, contrary to general belief. The reserve has declined a billion or two in the past five years, reflecting, according to some economists, the willingness of the United States to release the trade medium to foreign countries and make their trading position somewhat easier, if only in convenience. Even so, in 1954 the United States had well over half of the known gold reserves in the world (slightly over thirty-seven billion dollars).

When Fort Knox was established there was a general cry of "Why dig the stuff up and then bury it again?" The economics of the move are still obscure and debatable but in matters of world finance that enormous deposit has an undoubted moral effect that is probably worth the lost interest on the money that was spent to buy it; besides, the interest comes in full cycle —the government pays interest to citizens who pay taxes to pay it.

Out of one pocket into the other and back again.

The substantial good of the Rush, however, was not in technical fiduciary gains. It added one of the richest states of the Union to the United States effectively in a few years instead of a few generations. The agricultural settlement of the place was virtually concurrent with the exploitation of its gold and the agriculture grew almost immediately to be more important than the gold.

The communications with this place, which might have been an orphan state for a generation or two, were established almost instantly, first by the coach routes and as early as 1870 by a railroad. No one, of course, would have built a railroad to a place which had nothing to ship but perishables and no one certainly would have built one to haul gold—that was being taken care of quite adequately by coaches and ships—but the opening of California in this dramatic fashion suddenly gave the United States a Pacific seaport. It made the country bicoastal for the first time in its history and did it probably in one tenth of the time that would otherwise have been required. This country had the advantage of actually *having* California something more or less than fifty years before it would otherwise have been of any particular value to the eastern trans-Mississippian states, which at the time were, generally, the United States.

The inconsequential amounts of gold that were produced in the Gold Rush would have had the temporary effect mentioned in international politics and finance, but the plain fact is that the Gold Rush was the greatest publicity "stunt" ever staged, which is not unreasonable, since, in spite of the brief duration of its fireworks, it had taken a million years or so to prepare and it was worked out by the same agent who did the Grand Canyon and Niagara Falls.

It is impossible to beat Nature as an advertising agent.

A SHORT BIBLIOGRAPHY

In such a study as this, which is an appraisal or critique rather than a detailed history, a bibliography is likely to be more distracting than useful. One picks five lines out of some document or manuscript or volume; presents the reference solemnly in a kind of catalogue, and when the next poor devil comes along, he finds that the nickel's worth of gold was all there was to be found in five hundred pages.

Hubert Howe Bancroft's voluminous—if 39 large volumes are not voluminous the adjective needs editing—history of the West is the obvious original and factual encyclopedia of virtually anything dealing with western trans-Mississippian history up to about 1890. Mr. Bancroft had an advantage over the ordinary historian because he could employ as many as a dozen researchers at a time; a circumstance possibly less important than the fact that he worked at a moment when it was still possible to consult the folks who had "seen the elephant"—a phrase for direct observers of and participants in the American adventures of the Rush. He was able to talk vis-à-vis to '49ers, Vigilantes and the officials of early California; he also had access to documents which were destroyed in such disasters as the San Francisco earthquake and fire and by other attritions which inevitably occur to all records, on paper, gold, or granite.

This is no complaint, since Bancroft's (or his collaborators') researches tend to be more generous than critical, and one frequently wishes he would keep some of his moral reflections and classical references to himself; also, some of his anecdotes suggest that he occasionally took the line and sinker along with the hook.

For a time there was a cloud on his work because of his promotion of "vanity" histories—one bought so much fame in his books for so many dollars—but this has been put aside in the face of the enormous documentation he achieved or obtained. He is the Scripture of this particular place and period.

Theodore Hittell is more critical and a great deal more careful in his *California* though a little of the romantic quality of the episode creeps into his fine history.

The best modern book on the subject is Rodman W. Paul's *California Gold.* Here one's only objection is that the people have been omitted. One is not likely to find a better summary of the affair, excluding haemoglobin. The work is wholly admirable as a text; perhaps most admirable because it does not indulge in such historical license and comment as one finds in Herodotus or Gibbon. Whenever one finds that regular remark in Herodotus—"but to me this seems incredible"—one knows that he is about to encounter something juicy. It may be suggested that history is sufficiently juicy without ornament, but even a photograph needs a frame.

The contemporary accounts are usually mentioned as they occur. Such is George D. Magoon's "The California Journey," published in the *Iowa Journal of History,* April 1956. Franklin A. Buck's *Yankee Trader in the Gold Rush* comes in for frequent reference, not only for its beautifully naïve and objective attitude, but because it is so pleasant to find a Yankee caught off base—and sliding home, of course.

Bayard Taylor, Sarah Royce, Captain Marryat, etc., were simply doing pieces for the home-town papers. This kind of self-conscious journalism is not very useful. Unhappily, the thousands of letters and other manuscript fragments available in almost any large library are not much more useful. It is a sad reflection but it is almost invariably true that anyone starting a letter to some distant correspondent begins by thinking up lies. Not definite lies—associative lies. "Wish you were here." "The guano pies are wonderful." "Right here in the middle of beautiful Paris!"

They usually mean, "I wish to God I were back home."

And so it was with the Rush. Almost unanimously no one liked to mine gold—if he did he should have waited ninety years till a psychiatrist was available, probably in Los Angeles. It was a dirty, wet, repulsive business. The objective was two thousand miles east—a girl or a farm or a social success. So the letters are nearly all factitious.

The newspaper stories are almost unexceptionably incredible. It is not good business for a newspaper to traduce its location unless it plans to sell its presses. So the documentation of early California ranges from "Hey-hey!" to "Hell's bells!" with no chromatic interval.

My grandpa Duffield wrote his brother, "Don't come out here to be a crybaby. We have too many already."

So one is finally reduced to statistics, which, in spite of the ancient observation that figures don't lie but liars do figure, remain the simplest means of calculation for everyone but mathematicians. A probable number of people indulged in the Rush; an approximate amount of gold was produced; a number of social facts ensued. This does not include all or many of the factors, but it recognizes the important ones for 1849 and furnishes what is probably a reasonable calculus.

The background materials are sufficiently evident. It would be impertinent to offer formally such references as the Oxford English Dictionary (1933); the Thirteenth (and best) Edition of the Encyclopaedia Britannica and the dozens of standard authorities on everything from chemistry and physics to medicine and metallurgy—down to the op. cit. by the World (so-called) Almanac. As any worker knows, most of these things are merely on the corroborative borders of a research.

The justification for later-day reconsiderations is nearly always in assessments and later-day conclusions—not the author's conclusions but the ineluctable conclusions of effects which do not ordinarily follow too swiftly on an event or observable impetus. As I mention from time to time, perhaps tediously, the wealth, or medium of wealth, produced in substance by the Gold Rush was completely disproportionate to its effects or results, economically and socially. It was in iron that, immediately (historically speaking) after the Rush, there were much richer "strikes" made in America. These armed us with better shields than the soft metal.

It was such a drastic armament as was not repeated till a different refined ore fell on Hiroshima.

A good many of the casual references are noted in the text, and it would be pointless to cite the many fragmentary documents which anyone doing particular research can find in the Bancroft Library (unavailable to me by a few thousand miles), or the Yale Library (here in my front yard), which has plenty.

On routes there are four books:

Sherwood, J. E.—*Pocket Guide to California*.

American Geographical Society—Atlas of the Historical Geography of the United States.

Dunbar, Seymour—*History of Travel in America*.

Lewis, Oscar—*Sea Routes to the Gold Fields*.

Other materials are cited as they occur, such as H. F. Raup's survey of Gold Rush place names for the Geographical Review in October 1945.

Bartlett, John Russell—*Personal Narrative of Exploration, etc.*, and the *Life and Letters of Captain* (Frederick) *Marryat* as collected by his daughter, Florence, are more or less in the nature of setting—Captain Marryat died two years before the

Rush occurred, but he would not have liked it any more and probably far less than he did the California of his time.

Much the best *nearly* contemporary metallurgical work is:

Phillips, J. Arthur—*Mining and Metallurgy of Gold and Silver* (1867).

There are two authorities on Sutter, Sutter himself the more doubtful:

Zollinger, James Peter—*Sutter*.

Sutter—*Diaries, etc.* (edited by Gudde).

There are a hundred or so books on the color of life and labor in the Fields. Helper's *Land of Gold* and J. H. Jackson's *Anybody's Gold* are as good as any. I have leaned heavily on my grandfather's letters and reminiscences; to the best of my knowledge he was an honest man; better still, he considered the business in California as merely another enterprise in a life full of them, and not as a romantic adventure.

To the ordinary texts on the effects, historical and economic, of the discovery of gold I have added:

Bodin, Jean—"The Dearness of Things" (1568). (*Viking Renaissance Reader.*)

Barbour, Sir David—*The Influence of the Gold Supply, etc.*

Booth, J. P.—*Gold: A Delusion.*

The chicken-and-egg argument is interminable but probably Bodin cut close in saying that prices moved with the quantity of barter tokens.